...And There Will Be A Tomorrow

Eric Simpson

Copyright © 2012 Eric Simpson

All rights reserved.

ISBN-10: 1480296473

ISBN-13: 978-1480296473

Acknowledgments

My father dedicates this book to the memory of his beloved parents, grandparents, brother Izidor, Uncle Samuel, and his five close childhood friends: Hanzi Eiland, David Lessinger, Rudolf Spitzer, Sandor Spitzer and Ferencz Heimler. It is also dedicated to all the six million Jews and countless non-Jews who perished in the Holocaust.

I want to thank my mother, Helene, for all her help and support in preparing this book and for the encouragement of my siblings Janet and Ron Ames, and Michael Simpson, and. My father wishes to thank his sister-in-law, Seena Krizman, who is the loving sister he always wanted.

Many people have encouraged me to tell the story and, although tales of the Holocaust have been told before, each of the survivors has his or her own individual one to tell.

It is important that we reach as many young people as possible, so that information regarding that infamous time in history will be passed along. Perhaps by education, followed by understanding, we can prevent the recurrence of such terrible events. Sadly, we must acknowledge that genocide is still being practiced in several parts of the world today.

We have another purpose in writing this book. We would like to share Dad's thoughts and experiences with others, in the hope that they will believe that with determination and faith, anyone can survive the most terrible times. It is possible to pull oneself out of the depths of despair, to grow strong through adversity, and go on to make something good out of one's life.

Day of Liberation

April 30, 1945. The train, consisting of cattle cars with their cargo of some 3,000 human beings—almost 100 crowded into each car, had been standing motionless since the night before. About nine o'clock that misty morning, through openings in the train's siding, we could see a paratrooper descending to the ground! His uniform was unlike that of a German soldier. When he landed, he ran toward the train with a pistol in hand and called out, "Commandant!" A German officer stepped off the train and was taken away by the paratroopers

A few minutes later, olive-green tanks marked with a silver-star emblem in a circle and "USA" underneath emerged from a nearby wooded area and surrounded the train. The doors were pulled open, and we all stood there bewildered, afraid to believe what was happening. A soldier announced through a bullhorn, "You are free, you are now free! Please step off the train. Food will be coming very soon."

All the German guards were taken off the train by American soldiers who were part of the US. Army's Twenty-Fifth Infantry Division.

It is hard to describe the happiness I felt at the sight of those American soldiers. As I looked around, I saw people hugging and kissing and tears streaming from many eyes. A few people even bent down to kiss the soldiers' feet. I was stunned and found it hard to believe that we were really free. Our liberators had finally come. I was sixteen years old.

Growing Up

I was born in Szombathely, Hungary in 1928 as Gyuri Sauer, the youngest of three sons. My mother, Vilma Schiff, was born in Sopronkeresztur, a small town in Austria, where her family had moved from Vienna. My father, Sandor (Alexander) Sauer, came from a small town in Hungary called Tet. When my parents were married in 1918, they lived in the city of Sopron, where my oldest brother, Izidor, was born in 1920. My mother's family also lived there; my grandmother, Berta Schiff, her brother, Gustav Schiff, and her married sister, Frieda Goldschmidt. Frieda had a daughter, Liza, and a son, Ervin. I was very close with Ervin, whom I thought of as another brother. We visited each other back and forth and had very good times. Sadly, Ervin did not survive the war, but more about him later.

It was in 1921 that my father had become very dissatisfied with life in Sopron. He was not doing well in business, and had been advised to go further south to the city of Szombathely. He decided to make the move and planned to open up a hardware store, since he had learned a great deal about this business when he worked for his father.

At first he had very little money after moving to Szombathely, and so he contacted the Holzer family who owned a flourmill, a big hardware store, and a retail stationery business. One day my father noticed in the back of the Holzer's stationery store, that there were thousands of empty ink bottles just thrown in a big heap. He asked Mr. Holzer if he could take these bottles on consignment to try to sell them and he agreed. My father hired a helper to wash the bottles and put them in boxes; after which he took a few of them to Budapest to the Muller ink factory. Mr. Muller was happy to buy the whole lot, since there was a shortage of glass at the time, and my father made good money from the deal. That first break enabled him to establish his business on a firm basis.

A few years later Father made contact with the Manfred Weiss family, one of the wealthiest in Hungary and owners of a large manufacturing concern on the island of Csepel. Father asked for a credit line with them to sell their products, which consisted of hardware materials, machinery for the agricultural and construction industries, ovens, bicycles and other products.

After doing business with the Weiss company for about a year and establishing good credit, Father obtained from the company a wagon-load consignment of merchandise, which was sent to Szombathely. The consignment sold quickly, and months went by before Father realized that he had not received a bill from the Weiss company. He contacted them, and someone there said they would look into the matter. He heard nothing further, and so he went to Budapest. The company's credit department could find no record of the sale. Once again my father was told that they would search their records and be in touch with him. When my father contacted them again, he was told there was no such transaction on the record and he should just forget about it. Due to this strange bit of luck, my father became well-to-do and his business very profitable.

Two years later, after the family moved to Szombathely, my brother Tibor was born. The year was 1923. At the time, we had a governess whose name was Rozsi. Before I was born, we had a housekeeper named Anna who also helped with the children and, over the years, Anna became like another member of the family.

The relationships in our family were very close, except for my brother, Tibor. As a child, he was very contrary and rebellious and caused our parents a lot of heartache, but more about Tibor later in the story.

I had five very good friends as a child, David, Hanzi, Rudolf, Sandor and Ferencz and we were so close, that the neighbors called us "the six musketeers." We helped each other in every way and if one of us got sick, one of the others would bring his homework and let him know what happened in class. One of these boys came from a very poor family, but we made sure he was included in everything we did and never let him feel self conscious or embarrassed about his circumstance.

My mother's brother, Uncle Samuel, was employed in my father's store and, although he lived in a nice apartment, he spent a lot of time with us. I enjoyed being with him because he was my favorite uncle. On many weekends, my Uncle Gustav came to visit us from Yugoslavia, which was also fun. Mother always made the most delicious lunches; especially when we had guests. Afterwards, if it was a Sunday, I would attend the soccer games with my friends. These were good times.

Mr. Bonyhadi was the head teacher in the elementary school. I remember my first week there when he put me in a corner because I was talking too much. After school we went home the same way, so we often walked together. On the day he punished me, he explained, "Gyuri, I had to punish you because you are always talking too much. I know your family and you are a good boy, but you must learn to be quiet and listen more." I learned quickly enough because that was the last time I got into trouble in class.

It was mother's idea that I should learn the German language as well as Hungarian since both languages were spoken at home. Later on, knowledge of the German language probably saved my life. Mother also convinced me to take violin lessons with my friends and, although I wasn't the best violinist, I did have a good ear for music. If I heard a song once, I could always play it without the notes, but I studied violin mainly to please mother.

Mother did not tell my father that I was studying the violin. However, after two years of lessons, when I was able to play fairly well; one day during the Chanukah holiday, she asked me to perform as a surprise for my father. He pretended he knew nothing of the lessons. I played a Chanukah song, and mother and father had tears in their eyes. In the end, father confessed that the violin teacher had once sent a bill to the store by mistake. Now mother and I were the ones who were surprised.

Mother felt that, because we were fortunate, it was her responsibility to help those in our city who needed financial aid. There were several families that she actually supported on a continuing basis. When mother came to the store to help father, she handled the cash register. I saw my father smile as he watched her tuck some of the money in her blouse instead of the register. He knew that the money was for her numerous charities.

One day when my mother was walking in the rain when she saw a man who had torn clothing, and no coat or gloves. He looked as though he hadn't eaten for days. She approached him and took him into a clothing store where she bought everything he needed. Then she gave him money for food. By chance, there was a reporter in the store who had watched the whole thing. He told mother that, regardless of the situation in Hungary at that time, he was going to report the incident in the Vasvarmegye, which was well known to be an anti-Semitic newspaper. The following day, we read the entire story in the newspaper. I was so proud of my mother and I remember thinking that she was such a good and generous person that only nice things would happen for her. Unfortunately, this was not so and her life was to end too soon in a terrible way.

Almost every year before the Hitler era, mother attended a big fair in Vienna. She had some relatives there, one of whom was a necktie manufacturer who always sent father beautiful ties. At the fair mother bought us many treats from Vienna such as bananas and porcelain figurines. Once she brought me lederhosen, which was worn by people living in the mountain areas of Austria, Germany and Switzerland.

I remember my father as a very wise person, and one who always provided well for his family. During the summers he made me work very hard in the store. I had to sweep, wrap packages and then, when I received my own bicycle, I had to take packages to the railroad station for shipping. Sometimes the packages were heavier than the bicycle, and I had to struggle to push my bicycle all the way to the station. I didn't much care for all these responsibilities every summer and would have preferred to be out playing with my friends, but later on, I was to be very thankful that I had learned to accept responsibilities at an early age and that hard work had helped me grow big and strong. If I had been weak and pampered, I might not have survived the conditions I had to face in the years ahead.

Our family always had nice vacations. I especially remember one occasion in 1937 when mother announced she was going to vacation in Cirkvenica, a seaport resort on the Adriatic in Yugoslavia, and that she was taking me along. I was very excited because I had never been out of Hungary, much less to so exotic a place as Cirkvenica. That resort offered a cure for rheumatism, which was to bury one's legs in hot sand. Mother's physician had recommended the cure.

We went by train into the Croatian mountains. Then we took a bus down a serpentine road to Cirkvenica on the Adriatic Sea. Mother had rented a villa with some friends, and to me it was all very fascinating. The city was beautiful, the people there were very friendly, and the food was different from any I had ever had. One of the sights we saw was a huge warship coming into dock from the Island of Malta with British soldiers aboard. One of the lasting memories from that trip was a Bosnian hat mother bought me. It had black and red thread, like those the Muslims wear. Back home, everyone admired it. To this day, I enjoy reliving the memories of that journey with my mother.

During elementary school, father suggested that I start Hebrew lessons to study the Torah. I joined the class with my other friends. The study was very basic, and every Saturday we were tested. We goofed off a lot, and Rabbi Leitner threatened to lock us in the cellar. We thought he was joking, until one day when my friend Hanzi and I were jabbering away, the Rabbi did lock us in the cellar. To our amazement, we found people there baking matzos. They let us help, and so we had a good time, but we ate so many matzos that we got sick to our stomachs. That turned out to be the only real punishment.

Father had two brothers, Bela and Jeno, and three sisters, Julia and Szera and Sari. Julia and Szera lived in Tet. Sari lived in Szombathely. Szera's son Ocsi and I were very close and visited each other very often. Ocsi did not survive the awful times ahead, but we never found out what happened to him. After the war I met his sister Ili again; which I will go into later in more detail.

Mother had a sister living in Papa who was married to a merchant by the name of Rechnitzer. They had three sons, Dundi, Gyuri and Nandi. We visited each other back and forth and always had good times. We also had a number of cousins living in our city whom I saw very frequently.

I will never forget one of our visits to my grandparents in Tet. One Saturday morning, when we were all in the synagogue, I was astonished to see a very small person with a beard and mustache. I was so surprised that I called out, "Father, father, look at the little boy. He has a beard and a mustache!" Everyone stopped praying and there was total silence. People tried not to laugh, but I saw quite a few smiles; particularly on my father's face. My remark was an innocent one, since I had never seen a midget before, but I still had to apologize to the man.

We visited my grandparents very often and always felt very welcome there. One evening, our whole family was sitting around my grandparent's table having dinner. In the middle of the table were bottles of seltzer water, which they mixed with wine. Grandfather asked Izidor to serve him some seltzer in his glass. The bottle must have been defective because, instead of spraying into grandfather's glass, it went all over him and sprayed until the bottle was empty. Grandfather was soaked from head to toe. We all looked to see how he would react, and he just burst out laughing. Then we all joined him and could hardly stop laughing. I remember the scene as vividly as if it had happened today.

In 1938, many people started coming into Hungary to escape the German occupation of Vienna. The border between Austria and Hungary was within a half hour of Szombathely and so we had guests almost every Friday night and Saturday. We also received many letters from mother's relatives who told us about the bad things that were happening in Vienna. They advised us to leave Hungary because they were convinced that bad things would happen here too. However, most people, my parents included, felt that because Hungary was an ally of Germany, we would be able to survive until the war was over. How wrong they were!

Hitler invaded Czechoslovakia on March 15, 1939 and some of those who escaped, told us about atrocities that the Germans had committed against Jews. Father shook his head in disbelief and found it hard to accept that the Germans were capable of the dreadful acts that were described. The stories sounded widely exaggerated.

That same year, I went to visit relatives in Sopron and mother gave me a list of clothing I was to take with me. One day I discovered a couple of pairs of socks missing and I became quite upset. I went into the back yard where the laundry was hung to dry and searched almost everywhere. My cousins were watching me and wanted to know what I was doing outside at six o'clock in the morning. I explained that I had a laundry list from home and some socks were missing. I said I would be in deep trouble if I didn't find them. They all started to laugh, but I was very serious about it. One of my cousins wrote to mother describing the scene and told her how funny they found me to be. They also told her that she could be very proud of how responsible I was. This trait was to serve me well in future times.

There was a resort in Sopron at the Lover Hotel with restaurants and a large swimming pool surrounded by trees. My cousin and I went there very often to swim . On one occasion, I had to urgently use the lavatory. When I found it occupied, and a line of people waiting, I ran into the nearby woods. Suddenly, in the midst of my commune with nature, I was stung on the rear by a bee and the sting began to swell painfully. I went to the first aid station, where they pulled out the stinger and applied ointment. I was never tempted to use the outdoors for that purpose again.

Father was a very successful businessman by that time in 1939. The salesmen who came to father's store would sometimes stop at our house to have lunch or dinner with us, and father would often travel back to Budapest with them to buy merchandise. One weekend, when father and I were going to visit my grandparents, one of the salesmen traveled with us on his way to Budapest. I was a little bored when both men fell asleep, and so I started playing with a badminton racket. About that time, I saw a butterfly and began to chase it around the compartment. The butterfly landed on the salesman's lap, and I went after it with the racket, and in trying to trap the creature, I whacked the salesman. The poor man jumped up out of his seat yelling, "What's happening, what's happening?" The commotion woke father, and he took hold of me and said, "Gyuri, what did you do?" I replied that I just wanted to catch the butterfly—that was now quite dead. The salesman, who had recovered his composure, told my father, "Never mind, he's a funny boy. He didn't mean any harm. Just let him go." From that time on, that salesman always referred to me as that "schmetterling", the German word for butterfly.

My grandfather Lipot who was my father's father, loved to visit us and liked to drink dark beer, which I would get for him from the local pub. He always drank the beer with gusto. In the mornings, I had breakfast with him, but before we started the meal, he would take out a prayer book and ask me to pray with him. I would have hot chocolate; he had coffee and we also had some delicious rolls. I can see now the fastidious way he cut open a roll, put on butter and jam, and wiped his mustache. He did all these things with such enjoyment that I watched him just fascinated. He had a gold watch that played music on the hour. He would ask me if I wanted to hear the music, and he would hold the watch up to my ear. Then he would suddenly surprise me by gently pulling my ear when I least expected it, and we both had a good laugh. My grandfather and I had so much fun together and I loved him very much.

Grandfather Lipot loved my mother and whenever she went to visit my father's birthplace, they had good times together. Mother was full of fun and warmth, and she would ask him to dance with her which everyone in that small village would watch in amazement. Grandfather always looked forward to her visits. Unfortunately, my grandmother was overweight and not in good health, so she was not able to travel much and we didn't see her very often. I never knew my mother's father, who had died before I was born.

My brother, Izidor was very intelligent and heavily involved in studies. As a young man, he wanted to continue his education, but due to the Numerus Clausus Law then in force in Hungary, he could only make the six percent quota for Jews up to the university level. This quota determined the number of young Jews who could go to school, and it applied to all levels of public education. For Izidor, it was a big disappointment when he was not accepted in the school at Pazmany Peter University in Budapest. Instead he was forced to choose an occupation. After much thought and investigation, he decided to become a pastry baker. There was an elegant and very successful coffee shop in our city which was owned by a Mr. Fozo, who traveled all over the world picking up new recipes, and Izidor apprenticed with him.

When Tibor finished high school, he decided to become a mechanic. He worked for our father in the store assembling the imported bicycles. Occasionally, Tibor did other outside work to gain more experience.

When I was ready to enter high school, mother had her heart set on a very fine school, the Real Gymnazium, where some of the subjects taught were Latin and American and world history. Mother was excited and proud that I would be joining the same school from which my brothers had graduated. During the summer before I was to enter the Real Gymnazium, we went to register, but they told us the six percent quota for Jewish students was already filled. Mother was devastated and could not believe it. She said, "I live in this city. My husband pays taxes, and my other two children went here. Why can't my youngest son go to this school?" They told her this was the law and nothing could be done about it. Mother was so upset, she started to cry. I said to her, "Don't cry, Mom, I will go to another school, and I will graduate, so what does it matter?" "No, no", she said, "It's not 'so what?' This is a very fine school, and I want you to go here too."

However, we had no choice, but to go to the other public school to register. While we were waiting in line there, we saw a lady with her son who wore the same jacket I did in yellow and blue stripes. We noticed she was very upset. Mother went over to her and asked what was wrong. She said, "I wanted to register my son, but my husband is out of town, and he didn't leave me enough money. Now my son will miss school because I have no money for the registration." Mother took the woman aside and then a smile came over her face as she went over and registered her son. Mother had given her the small sum she needed, and as I had observed on so many other occasions, mother was always ready to help someone in need.

A new public school was in the process of being built, so the students had to go to the old one. Since there were too many of us to attend at the same time, we had two shifts. I happened to be assigned the afternoon shift from 1:00 pm to 7:00pm. This schedule lasted for six months, until I was transferred to the new school. Everything was brand new and I enjoyed that school for two years, until the situation in Hungary changed for the worse.

We had to go to Hebrew lessons every Sunday morning from nine to eleven. Rabbi Stein was a modern Orthodox, and told us fascinating stories about the history of the Jews. My friends and I loved to play soccer, and I remember that we would beg Rabbi Stein to let us go a little early so that we could play a game before lunchtime. He was a very understanding person who smiled when he asked us not to tell our parents. He explained that they were paying good money for these lessons, but he did agree to occasionally let us go earlier.

We played on a field which was very old and run down. By this time, the Jews were not permitted to use the larger soccer field that had recently been built. We enjoyed ourselves anyway. Since it was Sunday and we always had a big lunch which started on time, I had to rush home afterward. I would race to the kitchen to polish my shoes, because they would be very dusty from kicking the soccer ball, and I did not want Father to notice this. Then I would run into the dining room, and Father would ask why I was so red in the face. I told him I had rushed home so as not to be late for lunch. Father would smile. I am sure he knew where I had been and what I had been doing, and although he was not much in favor of my playing soccer, he never said anything about it to me.

Father's business was still doing well. He dealt with the Hungarian elite and with the contractors. Hungarian farmers came in every Tuesday and Friday and sometimes brought their produce to exchange for equipment. They would hang around the store and sometimes ate their lunch there which they brought from home. If I happened to be working in the store at that time, they would sometimes ask me to join them. Father gave a lot of credit to his customers because he never forgot his own good fortune and how he got his start. He was, in fact, very well-liked and highly respected by his customers.

Besides working in his business six days a week, father took paperwork home on Sundays. He was also heavily involved in the Jewish community. He became the treasurer of the community organization and, every Saturday night, he met with Jakab Ehrman to go over the books.

It was 1941, and things were beginning to change in school; some of our teachers were becoming overtly anti-Semitic. I remember one day I came home with a bad mark in physics. When I tried to tell Father that I deserved a much better grade, but that the teacher didn't like me because I was Jewish, Father became very angry with me. He thought I was just making up an excuse for doing poorly in this subject, even though during the previous two years, it had started to become more evident that such discrimination did exist.

There was a Catholic Hour held by the priests and the Jewish students were dismissed from class during that time for what was called "The Empty Hour". When we returned to class, it was obvious that the discussions that took place were not complimentary to us because some of the non-Jewish students were angry and treated us in a very hostile manner. By that time, the government was printing books which were part of the curriculum that contained lies about the Jews and leaned very much toward fascist ideas. The Hungarian government had unofficially supported the Germans from the early years of the Hitler period. School was becoming most unpleasant for me and the other Jewish students.

There were a few Christian boys with whom I was friends, particularly three of them. One was Gyula Polgar who volunteered to carry my books home from high school on Saturdays because, in the Orthodox Jewish religion, you are not allowed to carry anything on the Sabbath. Then there was Gyula Sarffy and Imre Hoffer who brought me up to date on what I had missed in class, and would give me the homework that I had to make up when I was absent during Jewish holidays. I often visited Gyula Sarffy's home, and we had good times. I also remember having nice conversations with his parents. They invited me to eat with them, and sometimes I would bring some kind of treat which my mother had bought for this purpose. When I visited Imre Hoffer his uncle, who belonged to the Hungarian Fascist Arrow Cross party, was very often there because he was otherwise unemployed. I remember the green uniform he wore. He never took any particular notice of me and so I enjoyed the visit at the Hoffers. In spite of everything happening in Hungary at that time, we remained good friends until, by law, Christians were no longer permitted to associate with Jews.

Most of the teachers in school believed the Germans were going to win the war, and we were taught that in history class. They told us that eventually the Germans would control all of Europe. This type of propaganda went on and on, and many were convinced it was true. In the movie theaters, films from German archives were shown of the prisoners that were captured and how the German army was being victorious in Russia and in the occupation of Europe.

We were all aware that Europe was unprepared for war and that the Germans who had built a big army, would breeze through Europe with their tanks against the horse cavalry that still existed in some countries like Poland. History tells us that is exactly what happened. The Germans had tested all of their equipment during the Spanish Civil War when they helped Franco to win and become dictator of Spain.

Suddenly, the Hungarian army requested that Jewish boys join Levente, which was a paramilitary group like the Hitler Youth in Germany. At the beginning, we had to go to meetings, where we had to carry out garbage, clean toilets, dig ditches, and do every kind of menial job. The Hitler Youth certainly were not required to do any of those jobs. Our high school principal, Jozsef Nemeth, a very fine person, made a deal with the military people that, instead of belonging to the Levente group, we should stay after school and take care of the gardening. This was arranged, and we were much happier to plant and water flowers than do all the dirty work for the Hungarian army.

In 1941, the Germans and the Hungarian gendarmes in the city of Ujvidek, which was near the Serbian border, committed horrible atrocities against Serbs, Jews and especially Gypsies. Leaflets and also newspaper articles were written about the "brave" acts that had been performed to kill all the enemies of the Hungarian government—a government that was infiltrated with fascists and ex-officers from World War I. Leaflets were passed around schools and pasted on lamp posts which blamed the Jews for everything bad that happened. We had a lot of German-Hungarian students who tried to make trouble by name-calling and provoking incidents and now there were many fights in the schoolyard.

Meantime, our lives went on, and mother continued to give a lot of fund-raiser tea parties with her friends in our home. The money from these parties went to Jewish charity in our city. Strange, but I remember one of the delicacies served at that time was hot dogs.

We had to go to school on Saturdays from 8:00am to 1:00pm, but we had to go to temple first, which meant leaving the house at 6:00am, even in winter when the weather was freezing cold. We always took some pastry and a thermos bottle filled with hot chocolate, which we had after prayers. Then, because the trip took another hour, we had to rush to be at school on time.

Saturday afternoons were always a pleasure. My five close friends and I went to each other's homes, played games and discussed what we would do on Sunday. The big problem facing us was, would we play soccer, plan a picnic or should we continue whatever we were doing that day?

During the summertime, our family and friends would get together, and with rucksacks, take the train to Koszeg, a beautiful mountainous area about a half hour from our city near the Austrian border. We would choose a place to picnic, and there was always a musician playing an accordion in the area. We would spend the whole day there, but the most fun was in the planning the Saturday before the outing.

There was also a place we liked to visit called the Seven Springs, where we went many times.

It was delightful to listen to the sound of fresh spring water rushing out of the seven holes from which it emerged to cascade down the mountainside.

When I studied the violin with some of my friends, we formed the Bluebird Orchestra. After becoming more experienced, we would perform on Sunday afternoons, for which we were paid. All this money went to one of the charities in our community. I didn't mind playing the violin, but I did not enjoy the practicing, which could not be avoided if I wanted to remain a part of our orchestra.

I finished high school with honors in 1943, which was not easy under the circumstances I have described. The atmosphere and treatment of Jewish students in our school had become even worse by that time. With the Numerus Clausus laws in effect in Hungary, most of us had to take on a trade instead of going on with our education. Some of my friends chose to become dental technicians. Father suggested that I consider the jewelry or fur trade, but I decided to go with my friends into the dental field. One of my friends at school, Martha Blau, who frequently went ice skating with me, was the daughter of a very skillful dental technician. Martha was not very good looking, but she was extremely nice and fun to be with. She often invited me to her home, and one day when I was there, I told her father of my ambition to learn the dental technician trade. He offered to take me as an apprentice with no salary involved.

One day I was at home from work quite ill, when the doorbell rang. I opened the door and there stood a very young German soldier, together with a Hungarian street person. They announced that they wanted a motorbike, which they had been told we had. I told them the motorbike was at the store and so they left. Father had an old Indian motorbike in the storage room that was rusting away. Later Father told us that when they saw it, they turned away in disgust and said nothing more. Later that year, the Hungarian government issued a proclamation to the effect that everyone had to turn over their bicycles and motorcycles to the Hungarian army. I was heartbroken when I had to go to the police station and give up my beautiful bicycle.

Twice a week that year, Polish soldiers who were prisoners of war came to our city and were permitted to do their shopping. I remember the square hats they wore. One of them frequently came into father's store and they became acquainted and Father showed him around the city. As they chatted away in German, the Pole told stories about what the Germans were doing in Poland, and father became very upset because, by this time, he had started to believe that there must be some truth in these stories. However, it was not long before people no longer had any doubt that the awful stories they were hearing were authentic.

Since Hungary was an ally of the Germans until the last hour before the invasion in 1944, the Jews there escaped the fate of those in the other German-occupied countries. The head of the Hungarian government, Miklos Horthy tried to keep the Jews in the country until, after the invasion, when he was forced by the Germans to get them out. Once the invasion had taken place, things happened very fast. The Hungarian transport of Jews and other so-called "undesirables" was the most vicious and horrible ever carried out by the Germans and the

Hungarian gendarmes during the Holocaust period.

The Hungarian Arrow Cross party had an office not too far from our apartment, but they were not very active at that time. Arrow Cross was a fascist group and therefore sympathetic with the German Nazis. Before the invasion, the Arrow Cross did not stir up too much trouble, but after the invasion, they swung into action as German collaborators. The most trouble just before the invasion came from the government itself, which was heavily infiltrated by vicious anti-semitic personnel. The gendarmes were usually in the outlying areas, but we did have some gendarmes in barracks in Szombathely. A few of them were Father's customers. These gendarmes were very strict with the entire population regardless of who you were. If you did anything wrong, you were beaten viciously. The head of the gendarmes was a member of the Arrow Cross named Col. Ferenczy. He was caught after the war and brought to trial with other Arrow Cross members and most of them received the death penalty.

A year or two before all this, around 1941, we often listened to Hitler speak on the radio. In his speeches, Hitler said he wanted to eradicate all Jews from Europe. We thought he was just a madman, and that no such thing could ever happen. Now, in 1944, we listened to the BBC in Hungarian. We would occasionally hear a professor broadcasting from England, who described the most heinous things the Germans had done in the occupied European countries. No longer could anyone deny what was happening.

Many times, we built a Sukkah in the backyard for the Jewish holiday of Sukkot. This was a wooden structure covered with pine leaves and fruits where we had our meals during the holiday. We would look up at the sky, and see American planes flying over Hungary. We understood they were bombing the Ploesti oil fields in Romania. I will never forget one afternoon in 1943 when we were celebrating this holiday, my Mother was having a conversation with the superintendent of our building, Mrs. Kampel, who was a very religious Catholic. Her exact words were these, "Look, you were born in the Jewish faith and I am a

Catholic, and I can see that things are going very badly for your people now. But nobody should ever change their religion, no matter what. You just stay what you were born in and God loves you." Of course, words such as these helped to convince father of his resolve to remain in Hungary at that critical time.

Life went on. I recall one morning when I found Mother combing her hair. I noticed a little bag next to her with toilet articles and extra clothing. I asked her where she was going. She answered that she had to go to the hospital for a check-up. She asked me not to tell Father and she would call him later. I didn't give it much thought, but at noontime father received a telephone call from the head surgeon who told him that they had removed a mole from mother's breast, that everything was fine, and that she would be home the next day. Father was shocked. Then I told him that I had seen mother getting ready to leave the house, but that she had asked me not to say anything before she called him.

Mother was always quite independent when it came to her health and she took care of herself without a fuss. But, when Father got sick, he was not a very good patient and could be quite demanding. On such occasions, Mother would tell him to get out of bed, saying jokingly that there was nothing wrong with him that a good laxative would not cure—which always made him laugh.

We started to notice that on Sundays or Catholic holidays, when the priests were carried on chairs through the streets chanting blessings and dispensing incense, Jews were no longer permitted to be on the streets during these rituals. Wherever we had to go, we had to cut through back alleys and take a circuitous route in order not to be seen anywhere near these ceremonies. If anyone in the crowd caught a Jew in the crowd, he or she would be beaten. If a gendarme was present, the punishment could be worse.

German Occupation

March 19, 1944, a cloudy Sunday in Szombathely, Hungary. Father had gone to the synagogue early in the morning, and my two brothers, Mother and I were having breakfast. I was preparing to go to violin practice with the orchestra, and before I left for the tram station, we looked out the window to see if it was raining. To our astonishment, we saw German troops with their trucks and cars and foot soldiers running through the streets.

Mother exclaimed, " Oh my God, what's happening? The Germans are in Hungary now. Gyuri, under no circumstances will you leave the house to go to violin practice today." Mother thought it might be a temporary situation, since something similar had happened in 1941 when the Germans marched through Hungary to the Yugoslavian front. However, there were so many German soldiers and so much activity in the street , that she became quite fearful.

We waited for Father to come home and when he arrived, he was very troubled. Everyone he had met on the way, was asking questions and no one seemed to know what was happening. Later we found out that Admiral Miklos Horthy, Regent of Hungary, had been invited by Hitler for discussions a few days before. While he was being wined and dined in Germany, the German Army just marched into Hungary. They didn't really have to invade the country, since Hungary had been collaborating with them for many years.

And so, on March 19th, the German army poured into Hungary from all sides and occupied every big city with no resistance whatsoever. The very first German soldiers we noticed were the SS troopers. At their head was Stardanten Fuhrer Becker. After they settled down, they occupied homes. Then came the gendarmes and the German security forces. The security forces were eventually placed in charge of deportations.

Hitler sent his representative, Edmund Veesenmayer whose headquarters were in Budapest. His principal task under Adolph

Eichmann's supervision was to handle the deportation of Hungarian Jews. He also directed the formation of an ultra-right fascist government in Hungary immediately following the German occupation. After the war, Veesenmayer was caught and given a 20- year prison sentence. However, John J. McCloy, who was the high commissioner in Germany, reduced this sentence to ten years and Veesenmeyer was freed after serving only five years of the 20 year sentence. The lenient treatment of Veesenmayer was never explained and to this day remains a mystery.

The heads of the new Hungarian government under Regent Horthy were Dome Sztojay and Interior Minister Andor Jaross. The two most vicious senior officials in the new government were ultra rightists, Endre Laszlo and Laszlo Baky, both of whom worked closely with Eichmann in the eventual deportation of 600,000 Hungarian Jews. Both of them were court martialed and executed in March, 1945.

The new Hungarian government's laws changed immediately, and officials began at once implementing the same policies for the Jews that existed in Germany and the other occupied countries. These policies included: "identification", which meant the yellow star, "isolation", which was the ghetto, "confiscation" which deprived Jews of everything they owned and, finally, actual "deportation" which was separation from homeland.

In our city, Eichmann's right-hand man was SS Commander Heinz von Arndt, who had his headquarters in the Palace Hotel. Heinz von Arndt was responsible for implementing all the new laws and regulations affecting the Jews. At the time, Father still had the business and we lived in our apartment, but day in and day out, the Germans with their Hungarian collaborators were arresting Jews as well as non-Jews. The latter were mostly Social Democrats who were suspected by the Germans of being Communists. Those arrested were generally successful people with businesses and manufacturing plants. People were arrested left and right at the railroad station and at the bus depot; many were deported.

In early 1944, some families in Szombathely received beautiful postcards from a German resort, with signatures of people who had disappeared. These people wrote that everything was fine, that they were being treated very well and there was nothing to worry about. This turned out to be a way of deceiving everyone about the deportations and to keep things calm. We later found out that, prior to being sent to Auschwitz, all these people had been given postcards to write, and then these cards were sent to the resort from which they were mailed.

I remember a very upsetting incident that happened a few months after Christmas. My mother had given the maid, Margit a gift of a pair of silk stockings. One day several months after, Margit was walking on the street when a gendarme approached her and asked her where she got the silk stockings, since they were a very rare luxury at that time. She told him it was a gift from her employer, Mrs. Sauer and he asked where she lived. The gendarme came to our apartment and accused my mother of dealing in the black market and threatened her with jail. Father was able to take care of the situation by using bribes, but the affect it had on my mother was very severe, and from that time on she seemed to change a great deal and acted very unlike herself.

One night, soon after this incident, Mother became very upset and I overheard her telling my father that she had the most terrible feeling about what was going to happen. He tried to calm her down, but after all that had taken place, she was convinced that the situation in Hungary would end very badly for the Jews. I was quite astonished to see her change from a carefree, happy individual to this pessimistic and dispirited person who no longer seemed to find any joy in life. I didn't recognize my mother—but she obviously had a strong premonition that even more terrible things were in store for us. Everyone began to feel uncertain, and fear spread throughout the Jewish community.

There were about 4,000 Jews in Szombathely, but that number dropped just before the deportations due to the fact that some of the younger people were drafted into the Hungarian Army. Some of these were sent to the Ukraine as slave laborers. These young people had to wear their own clothing and a Hungarian army cap and yellow armband for identification. The Jews who had converted to Christianity, some of whom had been practicing Christians for generations, had to wear a white armband. The Hungarian non-coms treated these people even more harshly, and they were forced to do a lot of hard labor, such as digging tank ditches and road repairs. Food was scarce, and a great many died before the Russians liberated them. Only a few of the draftees remained in various cities in Hungary and these had slightly better treatment. Also, a lot of people were coming in from the outlying areas to settle in Szombathely during the German occupation. This was another reason the number of Jews was constantly changing.

On March 29, 1944 in Budapest, the Sztojai government came out with a new law against the Jewish population designed by the Germans. The Jews were to lose their citizenship, and a solution had to be found whereby we were to be taken out of circulation and separated from the rest of the Hungarian population. The local SS commander, Heinz von Arndt, notified the Jewish community that they had to form a committee and that the SS would deal only with them. My father was on the committee because he was a successful businessman and a leader in the Jewish community. Other members included Dr. Ivan Hacker, Father's attorney, other prominent doctors, manufacturers and professionals. The committee chose Vallyi Mano to be its head, but because he had a gold medal decoration from World War I, von Arndt would not deal with him. Dr. Imre Wesel replaced him. Shortly after, the SS accused Dr. Wesel of something about which we never learned and he was deported. Finally, Dr. Hacker was put in charge of the committee.

He and my father had to go and deal with von Arndt, a vicious and difficult person who was in the higher echelon among the SS units, in charge of German occupation forces in our city. He demanded money, gold and other valuables from the Jewish community. He had a lavish household, and when he invited the committee to his house, he was often drunk and verbally abusive.

People in the Jewish community were very nervous about von Arndt, because his behavior was so erratic that they never knew what terrible things he was going to suddenly come up with next. When Father came home from some of those meetings, he was extremely exhausted, very nervous and worried about the demands that had to be met. Sometimes my parents talked until after midnight, because Father did not know whom to turn to and how to collect all those valuables to satisfy this SS commander.

When I was liberated and recuperating in the camp at Feldafing, which had been a Hitler Youth camp, it just so happened that Dr. Hacker was also in that camp. He told me many stories of things he and Father had experienced as members of the Jewish committee in our city. One day Adolph Eichmann came to Szombathely from Vienna and stayed for about a week. Eichmann started making additional demands, and the committee tried to explain to him that they had given almost everything the people owned, and there was nothing left to give. He shouted, "I will take fifty hostages and have them shot, and every day I will take fifty more until you meet my conditions." The committee was somehow able to calm him down, and a meeting was scheduled for the following day.

Again Eichmann demanded money, silver and jewelry. He said there were a lot of women who needed to be supplied with silk stockings and other luxury items.

On another occasion during the week he was in Szombathely, Eichmann told the committee, "You have too many sick people around here. Why don't you set them up somewhere and give them some food like bread with lots of butter and lace it with poison." Dr. Emil Danos, a member of the committee who was the physician in the school I attended, answered Eichmann, "I cannot do it, and I will never do it, even if you shoot me. I am a doctor and doctors are supposed to save lives, not kill people." Eichmann apparently found this statement amusing, and he started laughing and said, "Never mind, all these people are going to die eventually anyway, so just forget the whole thing for now." When the week was up, Eichmann had to leave before anything further happened, and we never saw him again—only the consequences of his evil work.

Father had another attorney, Gyula Weder, an older man who advised him on business affairs.

He was an exceptionally fine Christian gentleman, who was influential in the city government. He had a son in Vienna who worked for MTI, the Hungarian News Service. The son visited Szombathely only a few times; however, he sent news through his father. Once during these bad times Mr. Weder came to our house and he and Father went into another room for a long discussion. Both were extremely somber when they returned. He had warned Father that he heard it was too late for any of us to try and leave Hungary, and now there was nothing he could do to help us. By this time in 1944, the new laws were strictly enforced that forbade Christians to have any contact with Jews. Although Mr. Weder knew he should not accept anything from Father, he did take two gold rings for safekeeping that had belonged to my grandmother. We never saw him again after that, but when the war was over, Mr. Weder met with Tibor in Hungary and gave him the rings.

One night, I remember my father was very depressed and he said, "Something terrible is going on. Jews have been living in Hungary since 1840 and now the laws for us have suddenly changed. They are revoking our citizenship and taking away all of our possessions, and we are no longer being treated like human beings. How could this have happened?" There were no answers.

A few weeks went by before the authorities came to my father's store, since they were proceeding alphabetically according to the owner's surname. I happened to be in the store on the day the confiscating authorities arrived. I recognized my art teacher from the high school, Arpad Kovacs. He approached Father with a big book in his hand and said, "I am the representative now for the new Hungarian government. You must sign this property and everything on it over to the government, and then you must leave the premises immediately." Although Kovacs' back was turned to me, I approached him saying, "Mr. Kovacs, don't you know me?"—and, before I could finish, he interrupted with, "Sure I know you. You are a dirty Jew, and don't you dare to talk to me." Then he pointed proudly to the Arrow Cross pin on his coat lapel. I could not believe what he said. This was our teacher. He could not have said such terrible things. But he had, and I ran in shock to a corner of the store.

Father quickly came over to me and told me to keep quiet because he was afraid that I would stir up trouble. However, I was too numb to say another word. I couldn't believe that someone could change so much just because the Fascists were controlling the government. I was much too naive then to understand that people like Arpad Kovaks had not really changed, but had been given the freedom to express their true feelings. Some of those who jumped on that bandwagon and joined the Fascist party did so for economic reasons. Others were criminals who had been released from jail by the government, and roamed the streets with the German soldiers. Lampposts and walls were covered with declarations that the youth of Hungary should join the Death Head SS regiment.

Things continued to worsen. Even people we thought were our friends turned the other way; nobody would look at you or talk to you. Those that might have wanted to help were afraid. For the first time in my life, I felt totally isolated and could not believe that almost everyone hated us and that no one cared about what was happening to us. At age 15, I was overcome with tremendous feelings of anxiety and fear.

Starting April the fifth, we had to wear the yellow star, which was a prescribed size and a canary-yellow color. It had to be sewn tightly on all our jackets and overcoats. Just to make trouble, a policeman would walk over to you and put his pen between the stitches and, if it came loose, he would take you to the station house. Some people did not want to wear the patch and be identified as Jews, and many of them were caught in the railway station or the bus depot.

Shortly after, Jews were no longer allowed to use any public transportation. Then, a new proclamation was issued that Jews were not permitted to attend theaters, movie houses or soccer games and the parks were off limits. Under no circumstances could we fraternize with our Gentile neighbors or acquaintances. Also, as of May 3rd, a curfew was imposed from 7:00pm to 7:00am during which hours Jews were not permitted on the streets. There was a

Christian lady in our city who defied the rule and walked on the street with a Jewish woman arm-in-arm. They were arrested, taken to the police station and both of them were deported. On another occasion, a Christian high school girl went to a coffee house with a Jewish businessman. She did this to demonstrate her willingness to challenge the new rules. The police arrested them, and they were deported. A similar fate awaited anyone who broke these regulations.

The city officials, who were all Fascists by then, were planning where the ghetto should be set up. The head of the planning committee was Kalman Fordos, who was chief of police. Fordos, a vicious person who collaborated with the SS. He was the motivating factor in planning the ghetto. He was also in charge of bringing people from the surrounding villages into Szombathely for deportation. He was caught after the war and given a long jail sentence. Since my father was on the Jewish committee, he told us many of the things that happened in their dealings with Fordos, and I testified against him when I returned to Hungary.

The ghetto had been planned, but we were still living in our apartment and wearing our yellow stars. Father and the committee were constantly negotiating with the SS commandant. On May 5th, a new law was proclaimed that required the Jews to move into the ghetto which consisted of two large city blocks east to west and a half a block north to south.

We noticed the gendarmes that appeared in Szombathely at that time were not the gendarmes that we knew who had been there for years. The new ones treated both Jews and non-Jews very badly; beating people up for no good reason. In the beginning, these gendarmes were billeted in the outlying areas of the cities, but then barracks were formed within the cities. Some of the gendarmes in Szombathely were customers of Father's. When they were not harassing people, they kept to themselves. I found out after the war that these gendarmes were from the northern part of the country, and our gendarmes had been transferred further south. The authorities did this deliberately in case some of ours might be sympathetic and lend us a helping hand. So, there was a total rotation of gendarmes, and the new ones

surrounded the ghetto on all sides. The
gendarmes were also now in charge of
deportation, which I will come to a little later.

The Christian people who were living in the
area designated for the ghetto, had to move a
were put into apartments that had been
occupied by the displaced Jews. The moves by
the Christians were at the expense of the Jewish
committee. There were houses on the edge of the
ghetto, which had doors and windows facing
the street. These doors had to be locked so that
no one could leave and the windows had to have
dark paper over them so that no one could look
in or out. The gendarmes were constantly
watching to see that these orders were followed.
The ghetto also had four large doors about seven
feet high which were totally sealed. The
Hungarian newspapers proudly announced that
the Jews had been taken out of circulation and
would no longer enjoy the freedom they had
before.

To accomplish the move to the ghetto, the city
government appointed thirty people whose job it
was to go from house to house among the Jews
to make sure everything was done in the proper

order. Furniture had to be moved into one or two rooms and small articles had to be taken down. An inventory had to be prepared for everything we owned. The authorities were very strict that we must not keep gold, money, jewelry or anything of value. Some people tried to hide things before they moved to the ghetto, and some even took valuables with them at the risk of being caught. Father did the same, because he thought that after the war was over, these valuables would help re-establish our lives.

The city government gave 3,500 people only four days to move into the ghetto, starting May 8, 1944, to be completed by May 12th. The city was divided into zones and our turn came on May 10th, when a Hungarian official came to our apartment to oversee our move and, when complete, to put an official stamp on the door. Each of us was permitted one piece of luggage, and we could take only the most necessary medication, food and a few utensils.

I remember early in the afternoon we had to take everything down to the street, where a horse cart was waiting into which we packed our meager belongings. Mother was crying and Father was unable to say a word. I do not think I fully realized what was happening, but I remember how bewildered and unhappy I felt to leave our home and all our possessions. My brother Izidor and I helped load the wagon, then we all looked back one last time before getting into the cart.

My brother Tibor was not with us. He had been forced into the Hungarian Army's Labor Battalion, which did not save him from eventually being deported to the Buchenwald concentration camp. He managed to survive in the camp because the authorities discovered he had a good singing voice, and he was required to entertain the officers. For this service, he received a little extra food.

On our way to the ghetto, there were people who threw rocks and cursed us, and others called out in a taunting manner, "You are going away, and you are never coming back." Some in the crowd were convicts who had been let out of jail. There was also the indigent element of the city, who just followed the crowd. We did not recognize anyone we knew in this crowd who had come out to watch this tragic event. When we reached the ghetto, we unloaded our belongings at the house owned by Marton Holzer, who offered us one room in which all of us had to live. It was extremely tight.

We moved to the ghetto on a Wednesday, and that evening Father called Izidor and me to the basement of the Holzer house to help him dig a deep hole in the floor, in order to bury some trinkets and money that he had been able to hide from the authorities. We buried these things, thinking that the money would help us when the time came to move back to our home.

Finally, by May 12th, when everyone had moved to the ghetto, the Hungarian press came out and complimented Kalman Fordos for being such a noble and capable man who had accomplished the move of Jews to the ghetto so efficiently. Fordos was congratulated by the Hungarian government, and the city for having removed the Jews from society. Now there were to be no more yellow stars on the streets, and at last, the city was free of Jews.

Restrictions in the ghetto were imposed in three phases. At the beginning, fifty persons were allowed out between 11:00am and 1:00pm to obtain food for 3,500 people, but we were not allowed to go out on Sundays or holidays. Only the representative of the Jewish community could go out between 8:00am and 10:00am to negotiate with the SS commandant for any other business that had to be done. Youngsters like myself and young women were taken out to the houses of the German occupying forces, where we did cleaning and laundry. We also planted flowers in flower beds around the national Hungarian flag. Besides these duties, we collected garbage every day and did heavy physical work, like cleaning the army trucks for the Germans. We were taken out in the mornings and back in the evenings, guarded by gendarmes. We were permitted to take only a little food with us. We were not paid, therefore we were doing slave labor.

The second phase of the ghetto was implemented a week later when we were told no one at all could go out anymore. Some Hungarian farmers were permitted to come to the ghetto door with their produce on Tuesdays and Thursdays for two hours and people in the ghetto could purchase food, if they had money. We heard that the local Catholic bishop, Sandor Kovacs, protested against the conditions in the ghetto and tried to negotiate with the government to improve these bad circumstances. However, he was unable to accomplish anything.

At that time, Istvan Denes, a prominent Jewish attorney, protested the situation. He was arrested immediately and deported. No one could say a word on our behalf, and very few people could do anything to help, since the laws were extremely harsh and strictly enforced. One exception was our former grocer, Jozsef Palmai, with whom we had always been on the best of terms. One day, when father went out with the Jewish committee, he somehow managed to contact Palmai. Once in a while after that, Mr. Palmai was able to bribe a gendarme and throw some packages of food over the door to us at a pre-arranged time. This was dangerous for him and for us, but it was very helpful and we felt quite fortunate and very grateful.

I could not sleep in the same room with my family because the ghetto was overcrowded, and other people had been moved into our already cramped quarters. So I slept on the synagogue steps on a huge pile of luggage. During the daytime, when I wasn't taken out of the ghetto to work, Father asked me to help the older people. We formed a group of twenty and since the ghetto was so overcrowded, we organized the piles of luggage on the steps of the synagogue so that people could find their possessions when needed. We helped them settle into the rooms that were assigned to them, and tried to comfort and help those that were sick. I would go over to the house to my parents' room for some food and to wash up and rest during the day, but night after night I slept outside on the luggage. Sometimes I would go over to our family quarters to listen to some records which we played on an old phonograph. Radios were not allowed and there was nothing much to do in whatever spare time I had. This is how I spend my days and nights in the ghetto.

During the time the move to the ghetto was taking place, the Hungarian gendarmes went into the two largest hospitals in the city and chased out all of the Jewish patients, regardless of their medical condition. They were forced at bayonet point to leave their beds and march to the ghetto. People on the street turned the other way so as not to see the horrible sight of those who had festering wounds, women in the midst of labor and others who were dying. The suffering and degradation of these human beings was beyond imagination unless you had witnessed it.

On the day of the Sabbath, the second chief rabbi in our city, Rabbi Gusztav Gestetner, conducted the services. I remember standing with Father, listening to the rabbi. He was in tears when he said to everyone, "Pray, please pray, things are horrible now and our country is in total chaos. Pray for your country and pray for yourselves." Unfortunately, all the prayers in the world did not help. People walked out of the synagogue dejected with their heads down, and many felt that something even more horrible was going to happen. Others of us, myself included, felt that things were so bad that they could not get any worse, that we just had to get through these terrible times the best way we could until they were over. It was probably just as well that no one really knew what lay ahead for us.

Conditions in the ghetto grew more terrible. Disease ran rampant. The doctors were not able to help the sick, because there wasn't enough medication. The food supply dwindled. No matter how hard we tried to keep things clean, there just were not enough supplies. People wondered how long we could survive in these terrible conditions.

After the Normandie invasion in June, 1944, the Germans appeared to be losing the war. Now we believed things would go much faster, conditions would improve, and that the war would be soon over. We were wrong. The gendarmes began their reign of terror.

In the city of Szombathely, the police brought about 1,500 additional people into the ghetto, and the numbers swelled to over 4,500. Kalman Fordos always marched proudly at the head of these groups as they were being herded into the ghetto. Living conditions, which were already dreadful, became intolerable. After the war, I found out that even then, the newspapers had proclaimed that very soon trains would come to haul all the Jews away. They were called the Death Trains because it was known by many what our fate was to be.

There was a small building next to the synagogue that in better times had been used for social activities. The gendarmes decided to use this building for their interrogations and together with civilian detectives, they brought people there for questioning. The gendarmes took people from the ghetto in alphabetical order. They brought well-to-do people in for questioning whom they suspected might be hiding money or valuables. These people were merchants, manufacturers and professionals. The gendarmes would beat them with blackjacks on the soles of their feet and the palms of their hands. When the victims returned from this torture, they were bloody and swollen, and they could hardly move. There was no medication to alleviate their pain, much less to heal them. Sometimes entire families were taken in. If the head of the family did not reply satisfactorily regarding any hidden valuables, the gendarmes would use an electric current on his body in front of his family. It had to be almost as painful for the family to witness this brutal treatment as it was for the person being tortured. The gendarmes also enjoyed coming into the ghetto daily, going from house to house, looking around and taking anything they liked.

An announcement was made on June 25th that we had to be ready to move immediately to the Hungarian Motor Works, which was outside the city. We went from the ghetto through a narrow alley to a Jewish school. We had to stand in line in a big courtyard, where the men and women were separated and lined up. The gendarmes brought in mid-wives from other cities to examine the women, which they did in a crude and unpleasant manner.

We had to take our luggage and pass a desk where a man was sitting whom I recognized as a docent in the city museum. He had full authority to let us through with what we had or to take anything he wanted. When our turn came, I was wearing a beautiful beige sweater with a red design, which Mother had bought for me. He started to grab at it. Father pleaded with him to let me keep it, as it was the only warm clothing I had. Luckily, he did let me keep the sweater. We were then sent to the door, which connected with the city streets. The gendarmes were lined up, and now once again, we had to march through the streets where the normal traffic had been rerouted for the day.

Almost as soon as we left the door, a lady by the name of Mrs. Csaszar appeared. She had done the sewing for our family, because hardly anyone bought ready-made clothing in Hungary at that time. She looked at Mother and said, " I'm here and I want to wish you all the best and you'll see, very soon everything will be okay." Then a gendarme ran over to her and shouted. "If you don't move away immediately, you will wind up going with them." When she left, she was crying, and then she looked back and waved at Mother. She had a look on her face of utter disbelief as she walked away. Mother wondered how she came to be there at just that moment. The march took about a half hour, and it was very unpleasant. Again, people threw things at us, some cursed and some laughed; a few just looked the other way. Finally, we arrived at a very large sector which was the Hungarian Motor Works with a couple of old buildings. The gendarmes surrounding the area announced, "You will be staying here for a while, and we will let you know what is happening further."

The buildings were filthy and very old and the plumbing did not work. We also saw rats. Because of these conditions, which were even worse than at the ghetto, most of us slept outside. We tried to make fires and managed to cook a little with what we had been able to take from the ghetto. Mother had baked something in the ghetto that looked like muffins, but they consisted mainly of flour and water. Nevertheless, we lived on them for days. We had only water to drink. We were lucky if we could get some beans and a little fruit.

The gendarmes continued with their lists of people whom they would haul away and torture. Father came to me and said, "Gyuri, I am going to hide, and if they call my name, which you will hear, they probably won't find me because this place is so big". They never did call his name because in their alphabetical lists, they never came to the letter 'S'.
One day my friend Hanzi's uncle was taken away and tortured. They wanted to take his father, too, but he was very sick with

appendicitis. I remember seeing him lying on the ground being cared for by some Jewish nurses. It was a very hot day, and he had some dirty sheets spread on top of him because he had gangrene. The stench was unbelievable and he was suffering terrible pain.

Every day, I saw people who had been beaten and tortured, brought back on horse carts and just dumped on the ground. These sights were so awful, that I can never erase them from my mind.

Deportation

The days dragged on and then it was July 4, 1944. Every year I celebrate the July 4th holiday with my fellow Americans; at a picnic, listening to concerts and watching the fireworks, but part of my mind always takes me back to July 4, 1944—the day that the deportation of Jews commenced in Hungary.

Around noontime on that fatal July 4th, everyone was packed. We were herded to the railroad tracks and saw the train roll in and stop. We were amazed to see that the cars were not regular trains, but cattle cars. The SS officers and the gendarmes yelled out, "Line up and you will be counted, and then you will go into the train." They counted between 80 and 100 people for each car. Father had noticed that some of the older people were not able to climb into their wagon, so he asked me to help them. The gendarme standing behind us started to push me into the wagon with them. Father said, "He belongs with us. He's my son, and he just went over to help." The gendarme hit Father on the head with a stick, and fortunately, he was wearing a hat, which absorbed some of the blow. The gendarme shouted, "Go ahead with your father, you dirty Jew." When our turn came, we went into a wagon. Just before the doors closed from the outside, they handed two buckets into each wagon, one with water and one empty. They told us the bucket filled with water was our ration for the entire car for the journey. The empty bucket was for sanitary purposes. We learned that we would be going to a Hungarian workplace, where we would be working for the government. They closed the doors and the train started rolling. The time was about 3:00 o'clock in the afternoon of July 4, 1944.

That train ride was an experience so ghastly, that it is impossible for me to describe it accurately. I can never erase from my mind the things that I saw and heard. People tried to settle down to the best of their ability, sitting on their luggage and making room on the floor for the elderly. Mothers held babies and some had small children sitting on their laps. There was not enough room so the young people did not sit. We tried to stand against the train wall as long as we could, but after a while most of us had our legs give out, and when that happened we fell to the floor on top of other people. Most people tried to help each other and do the best they could. Food was very scarce, but we had saved some of the muffins that mother had baked in the ghetto. The most serious problem was the water. One bucket for almost 100 people did not go a long way. We tried dipping handkerchiefs and towels into the bucket to suck on as a way of making the water last. There were no washroom facilities of any kind. The bucket for sanitary purposes had to be emptied continuously, but there was no place to empty it. Then we had the idea to force open the wood floor of the car with spoons and knives to allow us to empty the contents of the bucket at least every hour and get rid of the awful smell. In order to pry open the floorboards, everyone had to move to one side of the car.

The train ran until the next night, when it stopped at the border of Czechoslovakia. During the stop, the gendarmes were going up and down in front of the train shouting, "If you have any valuables, leave them here, because you are leaving Hungary now." We all wondered what was happening, since we thought we were going to a Hungarian workplace. No one moved or listened to the gendarmes as soon we noticed German SS troopers surround the train and we saw that they would accompany the train from that point on.

As we reached the end of the third day, we noticed several of the elderly people were dead with open eyes. Conditions had been too difficult for them to overcome, and some may have just died of fright. During that night, some of the people started yelling and some began to tear their hair out. The worst part was that the SS guards would not allow us to get rid of the dead bodies, so they remained with us on that overcrowded train.

The train stopped to take on water for the steam engine, and the guards announced that one person from each car could fill the bucket. This task had to be done very quickly, and in the rush, we hardly had time to fill the buckets. We begged the SS guards to let us remove the dead bodies, but they refused. The stench was becoming unbearable. Once we had the bucket of water, we had to organize so that there would some for everyone. Again, we dipped a corner of our handkerchiefs into the water to conserve as much as possible, so that everyone would get a few drops.

The next day, I noticed that Father had a little pot in his hand. I watched as he reached into his pocket and came out with a bunch of Hungarian currency, which he had been hiding. He put the money into the pot and set fire to it. I was amazed. I asked him why he was doing this, and he said, "Look, we are now in a foreign country, which I suspect is Poland from what I noticed in the last train station. I don't think we will need this money any longer." I turned away, so that he would not know that I saw the tears rolling down his face. There was only dust left in the pot which he threw out of an opening in the train wall. At the time, I wondered why he had done it, but I believe that my father suddenly felt that it was very possible that we were never going home.

Conditions became worse. A few people actually became deranged, and some turned vicious and went completely out of control. The rest looked

very sorrowful with their heads hanging low. Mother cried and said, "Why are they doing this to us? Nobody deserves anything like this."
There was no answer.

One morning after five days, the train slowed down, and through an opening, I saw buildings and people running around in prison uniforms. There were others also in uniform whipping them. I couldn't believe my eyes. As the train slowly rolled a little further and came to a stop, I noticed a long building with a very large chimney. I yanked father's hand and pointed, "Look at the chimney, that must be a bakery." But then we saw dark smoke coming out of the chimney. Suddenly, a horrible odor hit the train, which in addition to the putrid air already in our car, was overwhelming. I knew then it was not a bakery, but I had no idea what that building was.

The train stood for five minutes before the doors were pulled open. Prisoners came to the train to haul the baggage away in trucks. My brother spoke to one of the prisoners, who happened to be Hungarian. He asked, "Where are we? What's going on here?"

"Don't ask any questions. You are not allowed to talk anymore, so just follow instructions. I can't talk to you."

We looked down at the platform and saw SS guards, recognizable for their skull and crossbones emblem. Most of them held the leash of a German shepherd in one hand and a cane in the other. There were a lot of prisoners with blue armbands with "kapo" on them. Some of them had an upside down green triangle on their jackets. We later learned that most of these kapos were prisoners from Germany and the occupied countries, who had been in the camps for a while. Others were volunteers from many different backgrounds, and a large segment were criminals, identified by the upside-down green triangle.

The majority of the kapos were collaborators with the German SS guards, and these kapos treated the camp inmates even more cruelly than the Germans, in order to receive privileges and extra food. After the liberation, many of them were killed by survivors before they could be arrested by the liberating armies. Those who were caught by the liberators, were tried by the military courts of the Allies.

All the kapos and the German guards started shouting instructions, "Get out of the train. Move quickly. Don't be so slow, just jump out." The wagon next to ours contained many people who had been let out of the insane asylum for the journey; others were very sick people, and a few were extremely overweight. No one in that car had been capable of keeping any order, and what took place there during the journey is beyond description and way beyond comprehension. When I jumped off the train and glance over, I saw mutilated dead bodies and body parts tumbling out and being hauled away. Those people who were still alive, were so hysterical that they were completely out of control. Some had gone mad with what they had to endure on that trip. The sights and sounds were so terrible that I could not take them in, and I turned quickly to help mother down from the wagon.

For no apparent reason, the kapos started beating some of the people, probably to show off their terror tactics. They announced that all the women with young children should go to the right and line up in rows of five. Men were to stay on the platform with the teenagers and also line up in rows of five. Mother went with her friend, Mrs. Breuer, to the right. This was the last time I saw my mother. Now, the men were lining up, but not fast enough, so the kapos and SS guards started beating them. I heard rifle shots from a little distance. Some people were killed on the spot.

Finally, we had to face a German officer. I can never forget his dark piercing eyes and the white jacket and black riding boots he wore. On his officer's cap, was the SS emblem of the skull and cross bones. We had to march in front of him. He never said a word, just whistled German opera tunes while he looked at each person for a moment and then motioned with his thumb -- to the right -- to the left. When Father came in front of him, he motioned to the right, and when my turn came, he asked me quickly in German, "Can you work?" Fortunately I was able to understand him and reply 'yes' in German, and he pointed to the right where I joined my father. My brother was also sent to the right. After this selection process, we were marched down a dirt road.

Much later on, I learned that eighty percent of the people deported were sent straight to the gas chambers. However, by the time our transport arrived, the Germans desperately needed slave labor to rebuild the German armament factories that were being bombed constantly by the Allies. Therefore, the able-bodied, including some teen-agers if they looked big and strong enough to do hard work, were spared.

Auschwitz Birkenau

I never knew how many people were selected to the right and to the left. But by night, all the people who went to the left were dead, because they were taken on a side road directly to the gas chambers/crematorium—the building I thought was a bakery.

While they marched us down the dirt road, one of my friends, David Lessinger, came to me and said, "Why don't you come with me? Some of us are going to a children's camp where they told us we would be treated very well." Father heard this, took my hand and said, "No, you will stay with me, and we will work together until the war ends." After liberation, I found out that the officer who did the selection was the infamous Dr. Mengele, and the children's camp was a special site for experimentation. I also learned that those children who escaped this fate were eventually sent to the gas chambers on the day of Yom Kippur, the most holy day in the Jewish religion. Father's instinct that I stay with him and the other men, instead of going with the children most likely saved my life.

There were about a thousand of us marching on the dirt road and, after fifteen minutes or so, we arrived at a very large barrack where we were chased inside. We were told to undress; keep only our belts and shoes and hang our clothing on hooks. There were prisoners waiting for us and, at the first station, they cut off all the hair on our heads. At a second station, they were waiting with razors to remove the rest of the body hair. The kapos who were to do the job were yelling and pushing everyone to move as fast as possible. It was pandemonium, and the result was absolute butchery. People were moaning and crying as they bled profusely. We were chased to a third station where there was a large pool containing a blue-green liquid, which had a very strong smell. We soon realized that it was a disinfecting bleach. The prisoners wore rubber gloves and used filthy rags, which they dipped into the pool, and then shoved these rags against our bodies to stop the bleeding. The pain was excruciating and now the screaming really started. I kept telling myself that this would soon be over, since nothing lasts forever, and I did my best to stay calm. Sure enough, at the end of this brutal procedure, there were cold showers, and the cool water helped to soothe the burning.

As soon as we were finished with the showers, there were other kapos waiting, and we were required to line up at barrack number 15, which was in the Gypsy camp. We stood there naked except for our shoes for an hour or more, and then more prisoners came with a truck from which they handed out our uniforms—a jacket, a pair of trousers and a beret. Everyone received a pot and a spoon. We were warned never to lose these utensils, as they would not be replaced.

A kapo came over and introduced himself as Mr. Ancsell from Romania, and announced, "You are in Auschwitz Birkenau, and this is an extermination camp." He pointed to the chimneys and added, "That smoke you see is from the people who have gone to the gas chambers, and their bodies have been burned in the crematorium." These words were so shocking that I just could not believe what I had heard. Once again, I blocked them out of my mind, which was the only way I could deal with such a horrifying statement. The kapo went on to say, "Don't ever get sick in this camp and, if you are lucky, you may be sent to another camp, but here, for every 100 people there is one aspirin." These words were to come back to me in the future.

The kapo left, and we went into the barrack to which we had been assigned. It was a large building, and we had to stand on the dirt floor. Two more men came in, and one of them introduced himself as Mr. Weiss, a former circus director from Vienna. He said, "We are kapos in this camp, and I want you to know that discipline comes first. So, if you have hidden anything on or in your bodies, anything at all, give it up right now, because if something is found when you are x-rayed, you will be put to death immediately." To make his point, he turned to the door, and two prisoners brought in a dead body on a stretcher. Well, that was all everyone had to see. I was astonished to observe people digging into every part of their bodies and come out with rings, gold coins and other valuables, which the kapos collected. They left quickly with their new riches, and we never saw those two around again. This was my first experience with con artists.

We were allowed to go outside, and we could see a few feet away, separated by a barbed wire fence, a Hungarian women's camp. We saw some of the women from our transport with shaved heads. Father recognized Dr. Hacker's wife, and he called over, "Have you seen my wife?" She answered, "I saw her being marched away with Mrs. Breuer." That was the end of the conversation, because the kapos and guards chased the women into the barracks for the night.

They told us that there were some wood boards, which we could use to sleep on instead of the dirt floor, and so we gathered some. As the night went on, I noticed that my father was still awake, but he did not say a word. I tried talking to Izidor, but he could barely answer me. We were so frightened that we just lay there awake all night, anxiously wondering what new horrors the next day would bring.
The following morning, we had to line up in front of the barrack, where we were given some foul-smelling black liquid to drink. Some people tried it; I threw mine out. Then we were marched to a large area on the other side of the camp where three trains were standing. After about half an hour, an SS officer came toward us together with a kapo to announce that he had

a list and, when he read your name, you must run and board the train he pointed out.

He started reading the names, and everyone did as they were instructed. When he came to Izidor's name, he pointed to train #1. Then my name was called, and he pointed to train #2. I don't know what was going through my head, but I suddenly walked over to the SS officer and said in fluent German, "Excuse me, sir, my brother went to train #1, and I want to go with him." The officer looked at me for a split second, reached for his pistol and hit me a hard blow to the side of my head. I fell to the ground and quickly realized that it was just luck he did not shoot me on the spot. Out of the corner of my eye, I caught a glimpse of the kapo walking in my direction raising his whip. I picked myself up and ran as fast as I could to train #2. At any moment, I was expecting a bullet in my back, but luck was with me for the third time since I arrived at Auschwitz. Î quickly jumped on the train. Father remained on the platform with the others who had not yet been called. I never found out if he was sent to train #3 or if he remained at Auschwitz Birkenau.

After I got onto the train, the door was locked and I found myself in the midst of strangers. I tried to make some room and sat down. We had gone along for about a half a day when I started to cry. I cried so bitterly that I know I had never cried like that before or again. The fear and uncertainty were overwhelming, and now there was no one whom I knew, not my father, or my brother or any of my friends. I was alone, and I did not know where I was going or what was to happen. I just cried and cried my heart out and I could not stop. I was still crying the next day, when a man from the back of the train came over to me and introduced himself as Mr. Mindszenti, a Hungarian. He said, "I want to tell you something. If you don't stop crying, I am going to beat the daylights out of you." But he said this with a half smile on his face. "Let's be friends and help each other. We're going to make it no matter what happens. Sit down and stop crying because you are going to make yourself sick. Now I want to tell you something, I am not even Jewish, but a Seventh Day Adventist."

As we were talking, I noticed another man get up and ease himself toward where we were sitting. He kept looking at me and finally said, "Aren't you Gyuri? Gyuri Sauer?" I answered that I was, and he told me that he was also from Szombathely and knew my family. He told me his name was Erno Geiszt. He was very glad to see me since he had not come across anyone else from our city and he was glad that we were together now. I introduced him to Mindszenti, and the three of us promised to be friends and to help each other in any way possible to overcome this awful situation. At this point, I was still sobbing, and Erno put his hand on my shoulder and said, "I know how you feel. I understand. We all feel the same way, but you are much younger than we are, and what we are going through is probably even more frightening for you. But we are all going to take care of each other and do whatever is humanly possible to get us through this." He told me he had watched in total disbelief when I walked over to that German officer, demanding to go with my brother. He said, "I thought, my God, he's going to shoot that boy, and everyone watching was horrified and holding his breath. What nerve you had to do such a thing." I told him that something just came over me. I had been losing everyone close to me and suddenly they were sending my brother away, and I just wanted to be with him. I said, "I know now that I was very fortunate not to be shot and I'm lucky to be here with new friends." Most of the other people on the train were from the eastern part of Hungary and they were so different from the people I had known growing up, that they seemed like foreigners to me.

By now, we were more experienced at handling this kind of transport situation which was made easier since there were only males on the train, no babies, small children or any of the elderly. We had learned how to allocate the water they gave us and to pry up the boards in the train floor to dispose of the contents of the sanitary bucket. We constantly changed positions, so that those who were standing could sit and try to take naps.

Now, at least, I had people who could comfort me, and we talked a lot about our homes, what had happened, the uncertainty of where we were going, and what might lie ahead of us. One thing we knew for sure, how lucky we were to be transferred out of Auschwitz Birkenau so quickly, since it was nothing more than an extermination camp. If you stayed there and were lucky, you were assigned to a work detail. But even then, you never knew when you would be selected at random and carted off to the gas chamber. This happened every day. With so many tens of thousands people coming into the camp, that is how they handled overcrowding.

We know now that after Hungary was occupied in the spring of 1944, 400,000 Jews were put to death in only four months between March 19 and July 31, 1944. That's how fast it happened. By then, Eichmann had made the operation of Hitler's "final solution" extremely efficient. But, although I knew I had been fortunate so far, I still could not stop worrying about my family and my friends. I cried again and again, until there were no more tears left.

The train guards gave out a little bread, but that was all we had to eat on that journey besides our small ration of water. The train ran for four days before it stopped late one night. We heard a loud voice announce, "Get out of the train. You have arrived at your destination. The doors opened up, we jumped off and were told to line up in rows of five. We saw a combination of SS and Wermacht (German army) guards. It was July 11, 1944.

Dachau Allach

We were marched for about 45 minutes to a camp where we had to go through a guard door. This camp had about 25 barracks. We were lined up and told to wait. Then a few German kapos arrived and told us that this camp was called Dachau Allach, a sub-camp of Dachau and administered by the main camp. They started counting people and told us we would be assigned to work details. Then they said that there would be no food that night, but the next morning when the whistle blew, we were to immediately line up in front of the barracks. The next morning, by the time people were counted and sent back into the barracks, it was more than an hour.

So far, no matter where we went, one feature was consistent; standing in line and waiting for hours. My barrack at Dachau Allach was #3, which was a very long one. The beds were three-tiered bunks. A single bunk was hardly big enough for one person, but each had to accommodate at least two people. The kapos told us how lucky we were because, in some of the camps, people had to sleep three, five, even seven to a bed in criss-cross fashion.

I noticed a straw mattress and one blanket on each bed, and in the middle of the barrack was a cast iron oven where a guard was seated. The camp was practically empty when we arrived. There were only a few German kapos there and outside the barbed wire were the barracks for the German guards. We fell into bed and the next morning, while it was still dark, one of the German kapos came in and announced that he was in charge of this barrack. He was wearing a red triangle on his jacket, indicating that he was a political prisoner. At least he wasn't a criminal like some of the kapos we had seen at Auschwitz. The kapo told us that everyone had to line up on the main road.

Then a nice-looking man, who was the Lager Eltester, the head of the camp, came in. He was a prisoner who also wore the red triangle with a "D" for Germany on his jacket. He stood up on a table and gave a long speech in German. He told us that Dachau Allach was not an extermination camp but a labor camp, that we should consider ourselves lucky that the barbed wire was not electrified, and that there were no gas chambers or crematoriums.

The Lager Eltester told us that we would be required to work very, very hard, and that if we slacked off or were caught stealing food, we would be sent to the main camp of Dachau and never seen again. Trucks were always lined up outside of the camp as a reminder that if you did anything wrong, you would be taken away immediately. He said that there were no work details yet, but that very soon we would each be assigned one. He repeated that if we did not work very hard, we would be branded saboteurs and treated accordingly.

He asked whoever could speak fluent German to raise their hands, which I did. Since I was so young, I was not picked as a kapo or a helper in the camp, but a lot of Hungarians and Czechs were picked. At that time, 80% of the inmates in Dachau Allach were Hungarians and the rest were Greek, Dutch, Belgian and French Jews. Later, we found out that there were some Frenchmen who had been fighting with the French underground, the Maquis. There were

Serbian partisans, some of whom were not Jews and also some Greek Orthodox from Yugoslavia.

We discovered that the camp next to ours had Ukrainians who had come to Germany as volunteer workers. That camp was much nicer than ours, with quarters that appeared quite pleasant and flower beds surrounding the area. Naturally, being volunteers, the Ukrainians were given much better treatment than we were.

That first day, we were called again to line up and wait in front of our barrack, which we did for another hour or so. After a while, an SS soldier proceeded to count everybody, which took even more time. They told us to stay in line and wait for our food. This so-called "food" was again the black, foul-tasting liquid. I realized by now that I would starve if I refused anything they gave us to eat, so I drank that awful substance because I needed something hot in my stomach. When we finished, we were told to return to the barrack and stay there until we were called out again later in the morning. My two new friends were in the same barrack in different bunks. We tried to make arrangements to sleep closer, but that didn't work. I also learned from the other inmates that, when you were given food, you must eat it on the spot, because if you tried to save any, it would probably be stolen. Thus, I learned some of the rules of camp survival very fast.

Before noon on that first day in Dachau Allach, they blew the whistle and we had to line up outside again, where we saw that trucks had arrived with food. They gave us soup with potato and cabbage peels, but the liquid was so thin it tasted like plain hot water. We were told that as soon as we finished eating, we could stand around. Since it was a nice sunny day, we stayed outside and talked to each other and tried to learn more about where we were.

We found out that there were Germans and Austrians in the administration building; some were communists, some socialists, and a few Czech kapos. We thought that the kapos here were not too bad. They yelled and screamed a lot to please the Germans, but no one was seriously punished, and we felt quite fortunate. But the situation was not to remain that way for long. We hung around for another day or two, and then the camp officials announced that we were about to be assigned to work details.

There was cold running water and big latrines outside the barracks, but the kitchen had not yet been opened. This camp was established by the BMW people and the Todt Organization. The latter was the German army's Corps of Engineers. Every night, we heard strange sounds and from a distance, they sounded like sirens. All night, they would go on and off, but in the daytime they stopped. At first, we could not figure out what those sounds were. Then we learned that they were building airplane engines in the BMW compound for the German Air Force, the Luftwaffe, which they tested at night.

The third day, we got up routinely, lined up in front of the barracks and, after receiving breakfast of the black liquid, we were counted. Our kapo in block #3 was a Hungarian named Rothholz, who was in charge of assigning us to work from a list. Various work details were assigned to a project known as Commando Kistengrube. The first such work detail to which I was assigned involved more than a hundred of us on a large construction site. Trains were coming and going continuously, and the minute a train arrived, we had to unload the gravel that was transported on it. As soon as the train had been emptied, the next train was there to unload. We never had a chance to rest. In the beginning, there were SS guards with dogs on leashes and canes in one hand. If they caught you working too slowly, they either threatened you with the dogs or gave you a beating right there. In addition to everything else, there were German civilians dressed in the Bavarian attire of hat and lederhosen, who yelled continuously and seemed to enjoy making things harder for us.

At ten o'clock every morning, these civilian overseers took a break and sat down to sandwiches and beer, while they pushed us to work faster. They threatened that, if we did not do the work the way we were told and were not quick enough, they would report us to the main camp. I was on this work detail for about a week when, one day, I began to feel very weak and almost passed out. It was very hot and besides the constant hunger pangs, I was terribly thirsty. I saw a German officer in a strange uniform—which was not SS or Wehrmacht—come out of his hut. He looked at me and said," Hey, youngster, come over here." When I came up to him, he pulled me into the hut, quickly closed the door and asked if I could speak German. I said I did, and he told me to sit down.

Somehow, I felt something good was going to happen. In a few words, he told me he was the officer of the day and had been brought in from somewhere else. He said he had been an officer in World War I and did not believe in the Nazi regime. He told me he knew who we were and what was happening and that he had noticed when I almost collapsed outside. He went over to a little bag that was hanging on a hook, took out a piece of dark bread and handed it to me. "Eat it and eat it fast," he said, "because if I get caught giving this to you, I will wind up a prisoner in a concentration camp myself." I ate the bread and thanked him. He went out and talked to a German civilian and their conversation sounded angry and the tone was argumentative. When I came out, the civilian assigned me to a different work detail, which turned out to be an easy one. I operated the handle on a very large cement mixer that had a diesel motor, and there was no physical work involved. After I was liberated, I tried very hard to find that officer, because I wanted to thank him for his kindness to me, but my efforts were unsuccessful.

I stayed on that work detail for another month, when it happened that a big construction firm from Munich—Sager & Woerner—requested prisoners to work a day and night shift repairing the railroad tracks. I was assigned to the night shift, which turned out to be very unpleasant. It was freezing cold by then, and the work was extremely hard. The guards treated us very badly, and most people on this detail did not last long. I found out that the kapo, Rotholz, who assigned me to this detail, was involved in Hungary with the Csepel factory, where my father was a customer.

I approached him and said, "Mr. Rotholz, you probably knew my father from Szombathely. He had a big hardware business and was a customer of Csepel." He said, "Yes, I think I know the name, but right now I am not interested and I can't do anything for you. You had better get back to work before you are punished." He was obviously showing off to the

Germans by treating us harshly. Whatever power he had, seemed to have gone to his head. I thought if I ever got out of this situation, I would try to find him. What I intended to do if I did find him, I did not know.

I worked on the night shift for quite sometime until I became ill. I had a bad cold, and knew that I had a high fever. I had heard that there was no sick bay, just a small barrack which contained ten or twelve beds for the very sick. There were also rumors that it was very dangerous to go there, because people who were seriously ill were often carted off to the Dachau main camp. Also, the kapo in charge was a former criminal who liked to beat those who were weak and ill. I had to consider what I was going to do, but then I started coughing very hard and felt so sick that I no longer had a choice.

I walked over to the facility that passed for a sick bay and, before the kapo could say a word or lay a hand on me, I said, "Look, I am a very hard worker, but I cannot continue because I am very sick and need help." This time being brazen worked to my advantage. The kapo was so startled at the manner in which I had confronted him, that he just stared at me for a moment; then told me to get into one of the beds and my temperature would be taken. I jumped at the opportunity and could hardly believe it when I saw white sheets, a pillow with a pillow case, and a blanket on the bed. My clothing was collected and they gave me pajamas. Sure enough, I had a high fever and, much to my surprise, the kapo brought me an aspirin and a glass of water. Then he shouted at me to take it quickly.

I thought back to Auschwitz, where they told us that 100 people would get one aspirin, and here, unbelievably I was getting a whole aspirin for myself. The food was no better in the infirmary since it was the same as we always received, but they did give out a bit more of it and the hot liquid felt good in my stomach.
I was in bed for two days and in the bed next to me was a Greek fellow from Salonika. He gave me a valuable tip, "You could stay here a little longer if you have a high fever, but they won't let you stay if it is low or normal. When they give you the thermometer, rub it between your fingers. This will cause the temperature reading

to go up, and they will think you still have a high fever." This trick was an easy one because they took the temperature under the armpit. I followed this advice and when the kapo read the thermometer, he said I was too sick to get out of bed.

After a few more days, he told me that, since I seemed to be getting better, he could use my help in the latrine. He said that I should stay in bed until he needed me. When I started cleaning the toilets, I did a good job, even cleaning the walls. One day, in my enthusiasm, I knocked an aluminum pipe loose and it fell off the wall. Water gushed all over the place. I was alarmed, because I thought the kapo would accuse me of sabotage. I had to report the break anyway, and in fluent German I described what had happened. He rushed in, looked at the flooding from the loose pipe and to my surprise, he smiled and said, "This is stupid, it's a rotten old pipe, and I don't know why the Germans put this in. Don't worry, we'll call the plumber from outside and he'll fix it. You have nothing to worry about. Now, go back to bed." I never could figure out why this kapo was being so kind to me. All those terrible stories I had heard about him turned out not to be true in my case. Once again, luck had been with me.

My friend Erno found out that I was working in the latrine of sick bay. One day, he knocked on the window and said, "Gyuri, I'm so hungry, I don't know what to do. I feel so bad. Could you get me a little extra food?" I felt terrible when I saw how weak my friend was. However, I knew that if I got caught stealing food, the punishment would be swift and severe, but Erno was really suffering from starvation. I took his pot, rushed in, quickly dipped it into the big container of soup, filled it and raced back to the window. I gave it to him and said, "Run, Erno, run as fast as you can because, if you get caught, it could be the end for both of us." I was glad I could help him even a little.

After a few more days the kapo sent me back to my barrack, and I was assigned to another work detail at a very large construction site for the German air force. I worked at shoveling cement into a cement mixer, which was not terribly hard; however, the machine turned over slowly and had to be fed constantly and it was a tedious job. Around the perimeter of the construction site were little barrels, each containing a pipe sticking out, and we could not understand what they were for. One day the sirens went off, which meant an air raid of which there were many over Germany in 1944. We saw the Germans loosen a screw in the barrel, which then released a lot of smoke from those pipes. The smoke obscured the entire area, so that the American bombers could not see the target clearly. The smoke had a very bad odor, and we had to protect ourselves from breathing it until the "all clear" signal came on.

The work there lasted for a couple of weeks. Then I was assigned to another work detail which turned out to be a more pleasant one with an unexpected bonus.

A German farmer had requested about 100 prisoners to do farm work and take care of the cows. My friend Mindszenti was assigned an outdoor detail on the farm, and I was assigned inside to clean out the stalls and fill buckets of feed for the cows. The first time I did this, I noticed that the feed looked like dry cereal and dry fruit. I decided to taste it and, to my surprise, it was very sweet. I was determined to get hold of some of this cow fodder, so I asked Mindszenti to watch outside and signal where the guards were. After I brought the feed in, I took my fist and knocked one of the cows on the nose. She let out a loud bellow and turned her head away, so I quickly filled both my pants pockets with fodder and signaled Mindszenti it was done. At lunchtime, I was able to dump the feed into our soup, and fortunately the German guard never noticed. This new source of food lasted for a few weeks and since neither of us got sick, the cows' feed turned out to be a good supplement to our meager diet.

One evening, my friends told me that there was a rabbi in the camp from the city of Cluj which is in Romania, and that he was holding a little prayer service outside the barracks. This was risky, and somehow the Germans found out about it and punished the rabbi harshly. They put him in the middle of the camp to dig ditches, which he had to do from morning until night. This punishment lasted for several months, and in addition, the guards beat him severely many times—probably the more so because he was a rabbi. We never could understand how this man survived all that brutality, but he did. I learned that, after the war, he went to Israel where he founded several religious schools and became quite famous.

We noticed that outside the camp there was an extremely large pit more than half filled with filthy brown water which smelled terrible. Whenever we came back to the camp from our work places, we noticed that the odor was getting worse. One Sunday, it was announced that everyone in the barracks, would have to line up outside the camp. The SS guards were waiting on top and we were chased down and told that we had to take a bath in the pit. There were hundreds of people in each barrack and the guards couldn't see if everyone went into the water, so I quickly looked around when I put my jacket and pants down, since we were instructed to go in naked. Then I splashed a bit of water over myself to look like I had been in the pit. I climbed up to the top with my clothing in hand and the droplets of water on my skin, and the guard let me pass to get dressed. Some people drowned because they couldn't swim and the water was very deep. Some choked to death on the filth and slime and others became very ill from the putrid water. This was just a little additional "Sunday Sport" for the guards in order to get rid of some of the weaker prisoners and demoralize the rest of us.

I have seen people react in many different ways to the harsh and dehumanizing life in the camps. Some walked around like zombies, completely dazed; some just fell apart and lost their sanity, while others became apathetic and lost the will to survive. Many of the intellectuals and creative people seemed to fall into the last group. My two friends and I talked a lot when we were in the barracks, and they tried to encourage me whenever they could. They told me the Nazi Germans were all criminals from Hitler on down and that their intention was to obliterate the Jews. They agreed that our situation was very bad, but that we must never lose our courage or our faith. If we did, they said, these murderers would win. We persuaded ourselves that we not only had to survive, but it was important to survive in the best manner we could. We did not want to wind up like those who had obviously just given up while waiting to die.

It was extremely hard to be positive under the conditions we faced and the constant fear of never knowing from one moment to the next, what could happen to you. The Germans did everything possible to humiliate us and break our spirit. On Sundays, we were made to watch the dogs being trained to recognize anyone wearing a prison uniform. They accomplished this by having an SS person wear a padded prison uniform and the dogs were taught to attack and bite him on command. Also, the SS guards marched by us, laughing, and would say something like this, "We are doing horrible things to you, and you are never going to survive this, but if by some remote chance you do, no one in the world will believe you when you try to tell what happened." Then they would punch some of us in the face or in the stomach and laugh again. We experienced such behavior every time they came to the camp. There was no avoiding these incidents, because we had no control. But some of us worked hard to control our own minds, and I did everything possible not to let all these debilitating events get the best of me.

After the last work detail, I drew a very disagreeable assignment at the BMW plant, which was about a half an hour from our camp. On the way to this new detail, I was marching with a Frenchman named Jacques, and since the weather was wintry and extremely cold, we had to hold hands and help each other. The wooden clogs we wore got stuck in the snow and it was very difficult to walk quickly with the guards chasing after us and threatening us with the dogs. Jacques told me fascinating stories about his experiences in the French underground, and we talked a lot during this difficult march.

The location of the new work detail was a huge compound with thousands of prisoners from all the different concentration camps. For the first time, I noticed Germans working there in very ragged uniforms that had a patch with a white circle and black dot in the center of it. I found out that they were former German soldiers who had not agreed with Hitler's orders. They were not trusted and instead of being kept in the German army they were put into the camps. We never had an opportunity to speak to any of them and none of them looked our way, because the SS guards watched them very carefully, looking for the slightest infraction.

I noticed that everything at the BMW compound was guarded very closely, because BMW was building airplane engines for the German air force. I was assigned to a very large building under construction, and had to carry heavy cement bags to the top, walking on narrow wooden boards. As usual, the German civilians and guards would yell at us to move quickly, and it was difficult to keep your balance on the narrow boards. We knew that if anyone was injured, they would be carted off to Dauchau. This work detail was extremely strenuous, especially so because we were weakened from the limited food rations and its poor quality. Those cement bags were almost more than I could carry, and I felt so weak, that I was afraid I could not continue too much longer. However, luck served me once again, and I was transferred to another area three weeks later.

One day when I was working in the BMW compound and had sat down to have my soup, an SS guard patrolling with his dog, stopped and looked right at me. I immediately stood up at attention and he asked me for my name. Then he wanted to know what my father's profession was and I told him he was a merchant who owned a big hardware store. The guard looked at me contemptuously and said, "That filthy Jew probably cheated everyone he could. He's another one of those people who doesn't deserve to be alive today." Suddenly he turned to the dog, gave him a command in German, but I only understood the word "fass" which means "grab". The dog jumped at me and took the lower part of my right leg into his mouth and held it there. I was terrified, and when I heard the menacing sounds the dog made, I thought he would crush my ankle, and then probably kill me. What seemed like forever was about half a minute, when the guard instructed the dog to let go. I got away with only a few teeth marks and some scratches, but I can never forget that slimy mouth with huge teeth and the horrible sounds that dog made.

Many youngsters around my age were chosen by the capos for what was called "house boys". After the war, we found out that these boys were being used for sexual purposes. Some of them became ill and suddenly disappeared, only to be replaced by others. Many of the children who were subjected to this deviant behavior were very troubled which showed in their behaviour. After the war, those children who survived, required a great deal of therapy, but many of these boys eventually displayed criminal behaviour. The American Army provided a great deal of counseling by chaplins and teachers; however, these efforts most often were not successful. Jeno Bacsi, a Hungarian teacher was involved in trying to help these boys and he wrote a great deal about this subject.

Suddenly our work load was increased and our food ration reduced to almost nothing, and we learned that some German generals had tried to assassinate Adolph Hitler. The guards made threats that we were all going to be killed, but fortunately, this new crisis blew over in a few weeks.

By now, we all had lice. Once you had them, they were very difficult to get rid of because they planted eggs in your hair and clothing. The hair on our heads, which had grown back, was cut with a Mohawk trail, but this did not help. On Sundays, we tried to clean ourselves, but to little avail. However, I was one of the fortunate ones who only had rashes that came and went, while people with sensitive skin suffered a great deal of pain and discomfort.

The area in which I worked at the BMW compound was filled with snow and the weather was very cold. So we were very happy when it was announced that we would be issued additional clothing. Meantime, our shoes had worn out, and they were replaced with wooden clogs. One Sunday, we were marched through the camp where the Ukrainian volunteers lived. We were allowed to take showers and, although the water was not warm, it felt wonderful. We received another jacket, trousers, cotton gloves and a beret. In addition, we were issued a coat. We were glad to get this clothing, in spite of the fact that it was not new and had belonged to prisoners since deceased. Much to our surprise, they handed out shirts, and I was lucky to get a woolen one instead of the usual cotton. There was a kapo at the BMW compound named Dicker from Czechoslovakia who constantly pestered me to give up my woolen shirt for a piece of bread. I refused. This was a very good decision, because this shirt helped to keep out some of the cold. However, he persisted in asking me if I had changed my mind, but I never did.

We wondered why the Germans were being so good to us with this extra clothing, but apparently it was necessary to keep us alive as laborers, since by then, German men of all ages and very young boys were in the army. At Christmas, we received a gift from Hitler which was a few sour candies and a pack of cigarettes which were called "Bregava" from Yugoslavia. Since I did not smoke, I traded my cigarettes for food. By then, we had our own kitchen in the camp, and some of the people who worked there were able to get enough food; however, they desperately wanted cigarettes. I traded my cigarettes for such things as carrots and boiled potatoes, which was a big help. This windfall lasted for almost a month, until I had traded all 20 cigarettes.

Once I overheard the Germans talking about potatoes that had been planted outside the barbed wire fence and, although the field was frozen, some potatoes were lying on the ground. Mindszenti and I volunteered to take out the sanitary bucket at night, which was a most unpleasant task. But we took the chore because we had to dump the bucket in the latrine, which was near the barbed wire fence. We had been told the wire was not electrified so, with Mindszenti as lookout for the tower guards, I reached across the barbed wire and grabbed a potato and put it in my pocket. We ran back to the latrine and quickly shared the raw potato. We were able to do this a few more times. If I could grab two of them, we shared with our other friend. Raw potatoes don't sound like much unless you are very hungry.

One day while working, I developed a very bad toothache. The pain became so severe that I could not stand it any longer. There was a Hungarian dentist named Dr. Pik among us who seemed to be a fairly decent person. I went to him to ask his help. He told me that the only thing he could do was pull the tooth. We arranged that I should come to barrack #4 later that night, and he would do the job. He sat me down on a rock and blindfolded me, which made me suspicious. But at that point, the pain was so bad that I just wanted the tooth out. He started work on it, but it took so long and hurt so much that I had to scream. After several minutes, he announced the tooth was out, and he took off the blindfold. I was happy the pain had stopped. But when I saw a screwdriver and a pair of plumbers' pliers, which were the instruments Dr. Pik had used to pull the tooth, I was glad he had blindfolded me.

We had a kapo named Knoll who had piercing black eyes and flaming red hair and a very hard look to him. He wore the green triangle of a criminal. On Friday nights, he came to our barrack and ordered people to gather around. He told us the most frightening stories about his days as a bank robber. He had been caught by the Nazis and sent to the camps many years earlier. He said the Nazis told him he would have to kill ten people a day in order to get a piece of bread. He described how he bashed people over the head with a steel pipe, then ripped their numbers off their jackets, and reported back to the Nazis for his bread. All this had supposedly happened years before, but we had to listen to his stories because we were afraid of him, and what he might do if we refused. Fortunately for us, one day, he just disappeared. I found out after the war that he was eventually caught and punished for all the grisly acts he had committed.

At the end of January in 1945, I was assigned to a work detail to build big houses for German civilians. It would rain all day without a stop, but we had to keep on working. When we got back to the barracks, we had no clothing to change to and had to sleep in the same wet clothing in which we had worked. The one small cast iron oven in the barracks provided heat for so many hundreds of people, that we usually could not get near it. Meantime, more prisoners from other areas had been brought to our camp. Now we had three people assigned to our bunk instead of two. But we did our best to make it through. I was on the housing detail for a couple of months that winter, and when it snowed instead of rained, it was not as bad. When we finished the project, it was early spring.

I was the only one amongst my two friends assigned to a detail in a wooded area to build barracks for the German volunteers. Compared to other work details that I had done, it was quite pleasant to be out in the woods in the springtime. At this stage in the war, there were fewer SS guards in the camp. Young Italian soldiers were brought in, some of whom were barely older than myself. They could not have cared less about the war, nor did they seem to harbor any negative feelings toward us. I remember one day when I was sitting eating my soup and watching them, one of these soldiers motioned for me to take his canteen and clean it for him. To my surprise, there was a little food in there, and when this happened several times, I knew he had done it on purpose. He only spoke Italian and we could not converse, but he pointed to himself and indicated his name was Mario and then pointed to me for my name. For the next few weeks, these Italian soldiers were our guards, and every noontime Mario and I played this little game where he handed me his canteen to clean, which always had some food left in it.

We were building barracks, because more and more German volunteers were coming into the compound. One day, the kapo in charge announced that we had to unload food supplies off the trucks, which had just arrived. After we had carried several big boxes to the loading area, we came back to the truck and picked up a rod that was hung with Polish sausages. My friend and I just looked at each other for a moment in disbelief. Then I motioned to him that I was going to take one. On the way to the loading area, I grabbed one of those sausages off the rod and shoved it down the front of my pants. When we unloaded the rod, I told my friend that I was going to the latrine to eat some of the sausage and that, when I came out, I'd give him the rest, and he should do the same. I got permission to go to the latrine, where I stuffed half the sausage down my throat very quickly so I wouldn't be caught. I don't know how I didn't get sick eating so quickly, but it tasted so good, I thought I was in heaven.

Sometimes, we had an opportunity to get extra food when we had to clean the volunteers' barracks and food was left around. Luckily, we never got caught, because the punishment for taking food—even scraps—would have been very severe.

A couple of months later, our kapo was replaced by another Hungarian kapo who did not understand a word of German. There was a guard with the Italians who was either an SS trooper or a Wermacht officer, and that one spoke only German. The officer was always trying to tell us what to do and how to do it. Every time he gave our new Hungarian kapo instructions, the Hungarian would answer, "Javol, javol", which is "Yes, yes" in German. Since the kapo didn't understand a word of German, the answer of "javol" didn't always make sense. The German officer cursed at him and called him "a damn Jew" and said, "Whenever I talk to you, all you can say is "javol". I don't know if you understand what I'm saying or if you're making fun of me." The officer was very angry, so I told him that I spoke German, and then I told the kapo to keep quiet and listen and not interrupt. He kept asking in Hungarian, "What's he saying, what's he saying?" The German officer was getting ready to beat the kapo with his pistol. Then the kapo stopped talking, and I was able to explain that the officer wanted a few people to go over to another work site, because more new barracks had to be built, and he should assign ten people to the job.

After that incident, I told the kapo that, since I had helped him out and saved him from a beating, from now on he should not pick on me or assign me to another place. He was a little reluctant until I threatened to tell the officer that he had been making fun of him. The kapo did not want trouble, so he left me alone.

Sometimes I was able to take things back to the camp. But I had to be very careful, because the guards always checked to see if your pockets were bulging. You were not allowed to bring back as much as piece of paper. My friend Erno was on the same work detail with me. He was marching in front of me one day trying to smuggle in a piece of newspaper. The guard saw it and kicked him all over his body. Erno was very lucky to recover from that terrible thrashing.

As previously mentioned, Sunday was always the worst day of the week in the camp. The SS guards had nothing to do for entertainment, and so they tortured us—every week. They made us run around the camp and if we did not run fast enough, the big German shepherds were used to chase us. These dogs were huge and their barking alone was frightening. Even today, when I see this kind of dog coming toward me, I tense up with fear.

When we finished running back and forth, they lined us up and picked out people at random. These unlucky ones were brought in front of everyone and stretched out on a wooden table. A big six foot, 250-pound Wermacht soldier named Sergeant Meyer meted out 25 lashes or more with a large stick, while laughing his head off. One Sunday during this selection, I saw one of the SS guards heading in my direction. He was pushing people right and left as he came toward me. I held my breath in terror, and then he selected a middle-aged man who stood just to my left; grabbed him and pulled him to the front. The poor man received his beating and collapsed before it was finished. Once again I had been lucky, but unfortunately that gentleman standing next to me was not. This scene was repeated every Sunday and the waiting while they selected someone to torture was another form of torment. I never was picked.

I witnessed a very sad incident one day when I happened to be in another barrack. I saw a man lying in a bunk, whom I recognized as one of father's customers from a small village near Szombathely. When he saw me he said, "Gyuri, I am not going to make it. I have terrible diarrhea and it won't stop. I don't know what's to become of me." Just then, a kapo from sick bay was going through the barrack with an SS guard. When they saw this poor man, they cursed at him and called him lazy, and beat him viciously. I could not bear to watch, so I ran away. I never saw him again, and I doubt he survived. One of the worst things you could have in the camps was dysentery, because there was no medicine, and you had to eat whatever food you received. Dysentery was the biggest killer in the camps, followed by typhoid fever and pneumonia.

In April 1945, when the war in Europe came to a close, we started speculating on when we would be liberated and by whom. We also were worried, because rumors were circulating that Hitler had issued orders that all prisoners in the camps were to be put to death. Such an order was, in fact, carried out in some of the camps. I learned afterward from other survivors that, in Camp Kaufering-Landsberg, in the Dachau area, prisoners were locked in barracks and then set on fire. Those who tried to escape were machine-gunned. When the liberators arrived at that camp, they found conditions to be the worst they had seen.

I was still working in the woods building barracks in the middle of April, when a large group of people were brought into our camp from the Warsaw area. These people were in very bad condition. It was announced that we were to be put on a train and transferred to another camp, since there were now too many people there—the number had risen to almost 7,000.

For the past two or three months, food had been increasingly scarce. We heard that the Germans themselves did not have enough food. We were receiving hardly any bread and the "soup" was now mostly water. We were on the verge of starvation. The Italian soldiers had disappeared, and in came German soldiers who were veterans of World War I. Some of these soldiers were so old that they could not even keep up with us when we were marched to the trains. By that time, most of us had very little strength left and some people could barely walk. I could see that my weight had dropped considerably, and I felt very weak and found myself shivering all the time. I could hardly drag myself down the road. I do not believe that I would have survived too much longer.

We were extremely worried when we arrived at the Karsfeld railroad station because we saw the Hitler Youth with weapons, SS officers and some Wermacht soldiers who were there to guard us. We wondered what was in store for us now.

The guards counted us, as they always did, 80 to 100 people to a wagon, gave us each a very small piece of bread, and the two buckets. Once the train was loaded, they locked the door. The train started to move. After a while, through openings in the wagon walls, we could see an airplane circling quite low, but we were not able to see the plane's markings clearly. It buzzed over the train and then disappeared. We heard artillery fire from far away, but of course, we did not know whose artillery fire it was.

The train moved backwards and forwards for several days, going nowhere, never reaching its destination. We did not know it then, but our lives were saved by a German officer on the train who did not follow his orders to take us to the mountains, where we were all to be shot. Whether he feared being caught or simply had no stomach for the act, his decision to delay that train saved us. The ultimate stroke of luck was that I was on that train and not one of the others where the inhabitants were not so fortunate. At one point, another train passed us at great speed. We saw through the opening in our car that the train appeared to have been machine-gunned. We saw people hanging out over the outside, dead and wounded. In the back of the train, we saw artillery pieces that were no l longer functioning and dead German soldiers around them.

This scene gave us some indication that something dramatic was happening, or had already happened. We also saw on the outside German soldiers without weapons running as fast as they could in all different directions, some with horses, some with bicycles, a few with cars. It appeared to be total chaos, and we were very frightened, because the Germans had said over and over again that they were not going to leave us alive no matter what. In a way, it appeared that something good was going on, but with all the turmoil, we did not know what to think. The waiting and suspense seemed endless.

The next morning, with our train standing still on the track, the American paratrooper and the other soldiers who liberated us appeared.

Liberation

We were liberated! We were free! I felt nothing but a sense of overwhelming joy and gratitude when we were liberated by the Twenty-Fifth Infantry Division. Now, we stood in front of the train where Red Cross trucks stopped and American soldiers jumped down and handed out CARE packages to each of us.

They warned us continuously not to eat quickly and to eat very little at a time because we could get very sick and even die after the long period of starvation. I followed the instructions and opened the package to find a pack of Old Gold cigarettes, cheese and crackers, a can of Spam, and a small bar of chocolate. Of course, I chose to eat the chocolate first and although I licked it very slowly, the taste was heavenly. There was also a metal can, which I struggled to open. I became suspicious when I finally did get it open and saw a mysterious white powder.

At this point, my only thought was that someone was trying to poison us. An American soldier watching me smiled, pointed to the can and indicated that I should give it to him. He took his canteen off his belt and put some of the powder in it, gave me back the can and motioned for me to wait. Finally, he came back with hot water from the locomotive engine, stirred the mixture and drank some, then handed the canteen to me. Since he had drunk some, I knew it must be okay. When I tried it, I discovered it was milk—the powdered milk used in the field by the American army. The taste was absolutely delicious; milk has never tasted that good since.

We wandered around, somewhat disoriented, from one end of the train to the other, everyone looking for familiar faces. I tried to find my friends and searched everywhere, but there was a lot of confusion. The area in the vicinity of the train was very crowded. There were more than 3,000 people shouting and running, and I just could not find anyone.

I finally recognized three other fellows whom I knew from the camp, and although they had not been friends of mine, the soldiers suggested that a few of us should stick together, because it would be safer that way. The soldiers told us to stay on the main road that the American army was using and not to stray to a side road, because there were still German soldiers roaming around, and they might shoot us. We followed these instructions very carefully. I was the only one of the four of us who spoke German; the others were from the Romanian side of Hungary and spoke only Romanian or Hungarian. We started walking slowly toward the incoming American army, which happened to be in the direction of newly liberated Dachau.

We saw soldiers on all the jeeps, trucks and tanks make the "V" for victory sign, which we did not understand at first. As every vehicle passed, someone threw us a bar of chocolate, crackers, cigarettes, and they did whatever they could do to help us. As we walked, some of the trucks stopped on the side of the road to build a fire with wood and gasoline to warm themselves, and the soldiers always permitted us to join them.

In a couple of hours, we came to a compound where American soldiers were guarding some SS women who were huddled together and crying bitterly. The soldiers only laughed at them, because they had heard that some of the women in charge at the camps had been even more cruel to the prisoners than the men. Now that the war had ended, they were not going to get any sympathy because they were females. Night came, and as we approached a German farmhouse, my friends asked me to speak to the owner, because it was very cold and we needed some place to sleep. I knocked on the door, which a lady opened, and she appeared to be frightened. She hastened to tell me that she was a good German who had never hurt anyone and she rambled on. I stopped her and said, "I am really not interested in your story. We won't bother you or come into your home, but we are cold and tired, and it's fine with us if we can stay for the night in the barn. We just need a place to sleep and get warm." She brought out a few blankets and walked us to the barn. We were so exhausted that we fell asleep at once on some straw.

Next morning, the woman knocked on the barn door and brought us a big pot of boiled potatoes and, in turn, we gave her some cigarettes and some chocolate. She was very grateful, since it had been many years since she had seen any of these items. We thanked her, said good-bye and went on our way.

The following night, we came to a big school where there was a dormitory that housed hundreds of liberated camp prisoners, but they had room for us, and enough food. I remember that some American soldiers stopped by, looked in and, when they saw who we were, they said, "Okay. It's okay now. Good-bye." They left and then more soldiers came and said about the same thing until I began to recognize the words. These visits continued until late into the night, and then we finally slept.

We walked for another day and arrived in Starnberg. The MPs on the perimeter of the city would not let us in because the place was already overcrowded. While we waited, some American medics came and sprayed us with DDT to get rid of the lice, and eventually, we were permitted to go into the city. Starnberg was a stopping off place for the American soldiers-- where they came to have lunch and rest before continuing on their way. As we walked through the city, we came across a very large store or what appeared to be a store, but was really a large warehouse stocked with all kinds of shoes. We saw people in there helping themselves and an American MP who was standing outside, motioned to us to go inside. I took a pair of black shoes my size and put them on to replace the wooden clogs.

I don't know what came over us, but we started running from one corner to another picking out shoes in any size, and soon I had five pair hanging on my belt. It seemed that we could not get enough of something, which was suddenly so plentiful, and ours for the taking. We left the warehouse and, as we walked down the street, a German lady approached us and asked if we would make a trade. She wanted shoes for her husband and son. We gave her the shoes, and she invited us to her home for a hot lunch.

Afterward, we continued walking and met some other newly liberated camp inmates who had not had a chance to change their wooden clogs for shoes. We gave them some of ours. We continued on our way and wound up in an old German police station, which was empty except for some civilians. They were sitting around talking, and they told us that they had just been liberated from Dachau and that they were socialists. We learned that a new police force would be organized with the help of the American authorities.

They invited us to join them in looking for a place to stay. Searching the local records, they had found out that there were many apartments and houses in Starnberg, a resort city where SS officers had been living very comfortably. They told us there was a house on the hill which seemed to be empty according to the records and suggested we go there and occupy it. We got the directions and when we arrived there, we found it open and unoccupied. We were pleasantly surprised to find an enormous quantity of foodstuffs, many of them luxury items.

We walked into the kitchen, where there was a storeroom with shelves of champagne, wine, Greek olives, salami and sausages of all kinds and bread. There were utensils still on the stove, which indicated that whoever had lived there had left very quickly.

We saw some pictures of an SS officer, which we tore to pieces in anger. It made us furious to see how the German had lived in this lap of luxury. Then we walked through the house and found suits and silk robes in a closet and dozens of shirts, underwear and pajamas in the dresser. We didn't look further because that scene made us furious. We decided to take baths and a shower. We burned our prison uniforms, and each of us picked out a suit and a couple of shirts and settled down to enjoy some of the comfort.

Since there were so many provisions, we motioned to the American patrol that was going up and down the street. They came to the house and we pointed to the champagne and wine and all the extra food. They returned with a small truck and took some of the stuff away, and there was still more than enough left. The soldiers were very friendly and motioned for us to remain in the house for the time being, which we did.

At noontime, we walked to the square where the American soldiers sat and ate their lunches. We needed some hot food, so we volunteered to clean their dishes. Although we were now decently dressed, they knew who we were by our prison haircuts. We also greeted them with, "Dachau-Allach, Dachau-Allach', and then they knew we had been in that camp. I remember that the American Army had four big barrels with fires underneath. The pots had to be washed and rinsed in all of them in succession to make sure they were clean. So we washed their pots and when we handed them back, they gave us some of their food rations—stew, beans and corn in cans which we heated in one of the barrels. In addition, they gave us cans of fruit cocktail. We couldn't quite take in the sight of food in such great quantity.

We went on like this for about two weeks, and then an American commandant made the announcement that all the former prisoners would be moving to a camp called Feldafing. So, the four of us packed our belongings in a little cart that we had found in the house. We took some of the food and some of the clothing and, after being given directions to the camp, we left. We walked for about a half a day. When we arrived, the American MPs told us we had to wait until the medic arrived. Once again, they sprayed us with DDT, and told us that we could not bring any of our clothing inside, even if it was new. No one would touch any of our clothing, and the Americans hauled everything away to be burned. We were almost certain that we no longer had lice, but we understood that such precautions had to be taken. They were giving out the Hitler Youth uniforms for us to wear, but because there were not enough of them in all sizes, some of us were given pajamas. The only item of clothing we were allowed to keep was our shoes.

When we came inside the camp, we were assigned to a large barrack that had been built for the Hitler Youth. There were two-tiered bunks with white sheets, pillowcases and blankets. There were pictures on the walls and a big beautiful bathroom. I felt as though I had entered a luxury hotel. They told us we would be staying there until things were better organized.

The next day we all met outside and Lt. Smith, an attorney from Chicago, spoke with us and told us he was Jewish. He had an assistant named Irving who was an immigrant from

Germany. Lt. Smith gave Irving instructions for us, which he then translated into German. Lt. Smith told us through his interpreter that, for the time being, everything was disorganized, so he could not say how long we would be in this camp. However, he assured us, there would be plenty of food, and very shortly, we would be issued some clothing.

Some of the personnel in the camp had been soldiers in the German army and were now Red Cross workers, carefully screened by the US. Army. There was a hospital in the barracks with American Red Cross nurses supervising. These nurses took down our names, asked a lot of questions, and issued identification cards, which were "DP" cards for displaced persons. They told us that we would eventually be permitted to emigrate to the country of our choice, but they could not tell us much more.

Time passed and we were moving around getting to know each other. I saw some people from the outlying area of Szombathely that I recognized from the ghetto. More people came from neighboring areas, since this camp was very large.

One day a transport arrived, and I was excited to see Dr. Hacker, my father's attorney, and Dr. Neuman, also from my city. They told us that they had been in the Landsberg Kaufering region. They hugged me and were very happy to see me, particularly since they had witnessed my actions when we were shipping out of Auschwitz—the scene at the railway station when I had dared to speak up to the SS officer who hit me on the head with his gun. We talked about the incident for a long time, and they made me out to be a hero, which at that point felt very good. Then some women arrived, and they were put into a separate camp. I recognized my mother's friend, Mrs. Breuer's daughter, Lili Fischer. She cried and said, "Gyuri, I never thought you would be alive." I also saw some people from the city of Sopron whom I recognized, and it was a good feeling to see familiar faces once again.

The food was getting better and better since it was coming from the US and there were many Care packages. Clothing also started to arrive, which they tried to distribute evenly. One of the displaced persons was a man called Max, and he was put in charge of our barrack. Max was a teacher who had come from Poland and he was a wonderful person. He held classes and counseled us and tried to help us believe that the bad times were over and we all had new lives to look forward to. He became our mentor. He also tried to establish work for us to do in either carpentry, electronics or upholstery. I chose to do carpentry.

I began to understand just how bad life in the camps had been; especially for those who had been incarcerated in the extermination camps for several years. I realized when I saw the others that I had been most fortunate to have been in a labor camp for only one year. When I thought about it later, it seemed as though I must have been in some kind of stupor for awhile after I was liberated. I just wandered around from place to place; not giving any thought to anything beyond satisfying my daily needs. Now I suddenly realized there were many things to think about, and decisions to be made, but the most immediate thing to be dealt with was to try and find members of my family.

Lists of survivors were now appearing, and they were distributed daily to every camp in

Germany. Every day, we saw high ranking American officers come into camp. Some had crosses on their jackets and others the Ten Commandments and the Star of David. To me it was astonishing that there would be Jewish chaplains in the American army. I thought it must be the best army in the world.

Also, civilian and army newspapers and radio correspondents came into the camp to interview us. They took our names, which they said they were sending to various newspapers in the US. If we had any relatives in the states, they asked us to give them whatever information we remembered, and they would try to help locate them.

One American army reporter spoke to me through an interpreter. I told him my name and my mother's maiden name and that she had a brother, Harry Schiff living in New York whom I would like to contact. The reporter took all the information he could extract from me and, lo and behold, two month later, I received a letter from my Uncle Harry whom the newspaper had located. He wrote that he knew all about my family, since he and my mother had been in close contact through the years, and that he had a son and daughter. He mentioned that when the opportunity came for me to come to the US, he would take care of me as he would his own son. I could start school immediately, or he would help me to do whatever I wanted, but he urged me to get to the US as soon as possible in order to start my new life. I wrote back that I would come as soon as I could, but first I must try to find my family. By this time, however, it was becoming obvious to me that many of my family members may not have survived.

I met a man from Szombathely in the main camp of Dachau who told me that he and my Uncle Samuel were together in Flossenburg, which was a penal colony. He said that conditions there were so horrible, that my uncle just couldn't survive it. Unfortunately, just toward the end, my Uncle Samuel had collapsed and died. This news was hard for me to hear because I had loved my uncle very much.

One day, the Americans announced they were bringing in a detachment of Hungarian soldiers, and this news caused quite a violent reaction amongst us. All night we yelled and threw things at them, because we thought they were the gendarmes who had treated us so cruelly. However, they turned out to be volunteers in the Hungarian army who had fought for Germany, which, of course, was almost as bad as the gendarmes. Finally, the MPs told us it was time to stop the ruckus now that we had had a chance to express our feelings. We did stop, but it was difficult to restrain ourselves, when we knew how viciously our own countrymen had turned on us. In the end, these soldiers were detailed to build a synagogue in the camp. I imagined that they found this task more punishing than anything we could have done to them.

The camp had a large social hall, and the American army set up loudspeakers and brought in a phonograph and records. They told us that they were arranging a dance under supervision for the following week, even though some of us were still wearing pajamas.

I remember the very first song they played was "Alexander's Ragtime Band". Every time I hear this song, it reminds me of that time of liberation. Ping-Pong tables were set up and actors came in and put on plays. The Americans tried to do everything possible to take our minds off the terrible experiences we had gone through, and to provide us with some enjoyment.

One morning when I awoke, I was itching terribly. I found white dots between my fingers and toes. This sight alarmed me, because I did not expect to be sick now when everything bad was over. I went to the barrack hospital and saw an American doctor. I told him through an interpreter that I was very worried. The doctor assured me that I just had a severe skin rash which might be the aftermath from the lice, but it could be treated and would soon disappear. He sent me to another room to wait for someone who would apply some salve as the treatment. I was waiting for an American medic when, to my amazement, a German Red Cross girl appeared who was young and quite beautiful. My mouth fell open so wide, I could not speak. She was not at all what I expected, and I was overwhelmed. I had not seen anyone who looked like that in a long time.

When she found I spoke German, we talked a bit, and she told me, "I used to work with the German Red Cross, and now I am working for the American army. My name is Lisa, and I am here to treat you. I will do my best to cure you as quickly as possible." She told me that her family had been bombed out, and she had no one now, but that she was pleased and grateful to have a job with the Americans so that she could do some good. I could not stop looking at her and felt greatly attracted, but when she told me to get undressed, I told her that I was embarrassed to undress in front of her. She answered, "You must take off your clothes, and I will be back in ten minutes." When she returned, I was still in my clothing. So she patiently explained that I had to get undressed, because there was no other way she could apply the ointment to every part of my body, and if she didn't do that, the rash would not go away. I had no choice. She went to a shelf and took down a large metal can and brought it over to me. I looked to see if the printing on it was in German because if it were, I would not have allowed her to put this medication on me. But the writing was in

English, and I could see for myself that it said, 'Made in the USA.'

When she opened the can, the smell was obnoxious. Imagine rotten eggs, gasoline, onions and garlic mixed together. It was dreadful. She took the ointment—it was a yellow color—and rubbed it all over my body, and I looked like I had jaundice. Then she sent me to a hospital-type bedroom where I had to be isolated for a few days because I was contagious. No one would have wanted to be anywhere near me anyway because of the way I smelled. I told her it was all her fault, and we joked a bit and had a good laugh. She said she would see me again soon and that I must not shower or bathe and that I had to stay in my pajamas.

A few days later, she came in smiling and, although the itching had stopped, I was not sure that the rash had entirely disappeared, but Lisa assured me that it was gone. Now I could take a shower, change into the fresh pair of pajamas she gave me, and I was allowed to rejoin the others.

I liked Lisa a lot and looked for every opportunity to go back to the hospital so that I could see her. We became friends, and I was able to help her out with chocolates, cigarettes and other luxury items. When she had time off, and I could leave the barracks, we went to Munich for a movie or a show. In spite of all the hardships I had endured during those formative years, I quickly regained vigorous good health and was feeling and acting like a strong and virile seventeen year old. I knew that I would miss Lisa very much by the time I was shipped out of the camp.

One day during that period, we were in the barracks when we were summoned to a meeting by American officers, who had arrived in jeeps with sirens blasting. One of the officers announced, "If you have any bars of soap left from the extermination camps, do not use them; turn them in immediately." I no longer had any of the greenish-grey soap, but many others still had some. These were collected in bags and buried by the Americans. It came as a shock to learn that the soap was made out of human fat.

After everything that had happened, this revelation was beyond belief. When I thought that I had used the soap, it made me physically ill. Later on, when I watched the Nuremberg trials, Colonel Rudenko, the Russian prosecutor, said that the Russian army interviewed a lot of prisoners in Auschwitz who testified that the SS had used many parts of the human body to make soap, fertilizer and other products. It was incomprehensible to me that any human being could have committed such barbaric acts on another human being, but such things did happen and were documented. To this day, it is still hard to accept and many people do not.

Another day, we were told that some high ranking officers would be visiting the camp to see the survivors for themselves and to hear our stories. A lot of jeeps came, and we saw silver stars on the officers' shoulders, which indicated the rank of general in the American army. One of the officers had a circle of five stars on his shoulders. He wore a dress uniform and was surrounded by MPs. It was General of the Army Dwight D. Eisenhower. His rank was the equivalent of the European "Field Marshal".

General Eisenhower was smiling as he told us that he hoped a lot of us would come to the US and begin to enjoy a good life once again. Quite spontaneously, we formed a big circle with our hands on each others' shoulders. General Eisenhower was in the middle of the circle and danced around with us. I thought to myself that this was the big general of the US army who had been in charge of the Normandy invasion, and it was unbelievable that he would join us like that and show so much concern for us. Once again, we were being treated like human beings for whom others cared. I will always cherish the memory of that day.

From 1945 into 1946, we really did not need any money. All the transportation was free to us anywhere we wanted to go. Sometimes the American trucks would stop for us and we could hitchhike a ride. It was helpful if we had cigarettes or chocolates to barter for most other items that we wanted. These commodities were in big demand in Germany after the war and actually had more value than money. I had plenty of cigarettes to exchange, since I still did not smoke. We received food and clothing in the displaced persons camp; therefore, I needed very little else.

I was in Camp Feldafing until 1946 until many more people were brought in and it became overcrowded and some of us were transferred to another camp. The authorities compiled a list, and I was on that list. We were told to pack our bags. and the next day the US Army trucks arrived. They said the camp we were going to—Fohrenwald—would be very comfortable and only a half hour away. When we arrived at Fohrenwald people were already there. The housing consisted of individual units that had been built for volunteer workers who had come to Germany during the war. Each of the houses had two or three bedrooms, a bathroom and a washroom, and was uniquely styled. Little streets were running through the camp, which was surrounded by woods. Each house was marked with a number. That housing area had the look of a quaint and picturesque village out of a story book.

I was together with a few friends from Camp Feldafing, and we shared one of the units where we stayed for a while. We had plenty to eat and additional food came in regularly. The people in charge of the camp told us it was not good for us to be idle, and so we were taken into the woods and taught how to chop firewood. This activity compared to the kind of work we had been doing was easy and fun. When we returned at the end of the day, we went to a movie or the theater. They told us we might also have the opportunity to learn a profession and perhaps work in the army motor pool.

In Camp Fohrenwald, I also met some people from Szombathely who had been liberated, and they told me that those who had gone back to Hungary, were now having to escape from the Communists if they wanted to leave there. I learned that my brother Tibor was living there and had opened a small hardware store. I was very excited and happy to know that someone from our family had survived. I wanted to get in touch with him right away and ask him to come to the American Zone so that we could go to America together, but communication was not easy at the time.

Meantime, I was still heavily involved in the search for my parents which was looking more hopeless as time wore on. To my sorrow, I already had learned from Dr. Hacker that Izidor did not make it. He told me that my brother had gotten sick because of his asthma and died just before liberation. I was not comfortable with this story, and for some reason, often wondered if it was the true story. Many years later in 1987, on a business trip from the US to Vienna, I visited Dr. Hacker who was the head of the Jewish community in that city. I asked him if the story he told me about Izidore was really what happened to him. He turned to me with a sad look in his eyes and said, "I didn't tell you the truth when I first saw you in the camp, because I knew it would be very hard for you to hear at that time. Your brother was a cook for the French Foreign Legionnaires regiment in Camp Kaufering-Landsberg, and seven days before liberation, the commandant ordered that the legionnaires—your brother among them—be taken out to the woods and machine-gunned." I was shocked and very sad to think how close Izidor had come to liberation—this brother who had been such a good and special person; whom I had loved so very much.

One day, I noticed my cousin Ili Deutsch's name on a survivor's list. She was my father's sister's daughter, and she was living in a city called

Eschwege. I went to the Red Cross office to find out how to get in touch with her. They took my name and said they would contact her for me and let me know.

I was still in the camp a few weeks later, when a gentleman approached me and asked if I was Ili Deutsch's cousin, and introduced himself as Mr. Heimovits. He told me that Ili was living in a very nice and large house with thirty other young girls. He said the person in charge of the house was Miriam Krakauer who happened to be from the same village as my father. Heimovics said that if I wanted to visit Ili, he would take me there the following week. He said he was sure I would like Eschwege, since it was a lovely city, and he also mentioned that my cousin would be happy if I would come and stay there. I decided that I had nothing to lose, and now I had found another relative who had survived. So, I gathered my things, said good-byes to my friends and told them I might not return.

The trip required various changes of trains until we reached Eschwege. We found the house at Louisenstrasse 21, and it seemed very grand indeed. The previous owners had been accused of Nazi collaboration, and the house had been taken away from them. As I had been told, twenty-five to thirty young girls were living there under Red Cross supervision. Another Jewish organization visited regularly to see that everything was in order, that they had sufficient food and clothing, and that the girls lived well, although with strict rules. Some of the girls had found relatives, who were offered adjacent housing. The American army gave us permission to stay in one of these houses, because we were not permitted to live in the house with the girls. But we spent most of the time with them, and we celebrated the Jewish holidays together. Once again, it felt more like being with family.

While I was in Eschwege, another gentleman appeared, a Mr. Samuel Ragendorfer, who had married my father's other sister. He told me he had just come from Szombathely and had seen Tibor. He advised me to go there and try to persuade Tibor to go the US. I had no desire to return to Hungary, but I sent Tibor a letter with my picture. He answered that he intended to live there for the time being to get things back in order. He wrote that he had been sick for a while but was now recovered, and he added that he was getting married and could not leave Szombathely at that time. He suggested that I come there for a while. I debated with myself, but the more I thought about it, the less I felt like going back. Then my conscience began to bother me, and I thought I should at least go for a visit. I had a great deal of trouble making up my mind and I went back and forth with my decision.

During my stay in Eschwege, I met up with two brothers from Szombathely, Ocsi and Bandi Kallus. As a child, Bandi had been quite wild. I remember he ran away from home several times and gave his parents a very rough time. He told me tearfully that when he was in the camp, he often thought the first thing he would do when he saw his parents again would be to apologize for his bad behavior and assure them of how much he loved them. Now this could never happen, because his parents were never coming back. He was twenty-two years old, and he looked like an unhappy and bewildered child when he told me this. I realized then that many of us would never have the opportunity to say the things we had neglected to say, or do the things we never had a chance to do with the people who were never coming home.

I lived very well in Eschwege, and I became acquainted with a lot of people who were coming into the city. One of the girls in the house had a distant relative in the US who was a food manufacturer. He sent packages every month with all kinds of wonderful things. We received numerous visitors from the United States, and the US army. Several Jewish chaplains also came and interviewed us. For a while, I felt as though I was part of a large family, and then things started to change.

Some of the girls met men and a few marriages took place; including my cousin Ili who immigrated to the US after she married. Others also began to emigrate, some even went to Palestine. Miriam Krakauer married a rabbi, and she was one of the last ones who remained in the house. She told me, "Gyuri, I knew your father very well, and if you are not going back to Hungary, why don't you come with us? We are going to a small city called Zalsheim near Frankfurt, where my husband has been appointed rabbi." I thought it over and agreed to go for a while. A friend of mine, Alter Heimovits joined us when we all moved to Zalsheim. Miriam and her husband had a large home there, and Alter and I shared a room while we decided what we were going to do. It was a good life, especially since I was still able to go into Frankfurt and trade my cigarettes and chocolate for going to the movies, the zoo and traveling on the train.

But, once again, I began thinking that I should go back to Hungary. First I registered at the American Consulate, where it had been announced that people between the ages of sixteen and twenty-two could go to the US, if they were in good health. I was one of the first to enter the Consulate, because I had seen a flyer in the DP camp. A lengthy questionnaire had to be completed, after which the consulate sent all the applicants to a doctor who was an older German appointed by the consulate to help speed up examinations. He checked me over and pronounced me in good health. After the exam, we spoke in German for a long time. He told me about his family and said, "If I were Jewish, the only place I would go would be to Palestine. Why don't you go there and help other

Jews who have survived this terrible time? Maybe one day you will have your own country." I told him that I had a childhood dream to go to the US, and now that I have found an uncle who will help me there, nothing can change my mind.

A couple of weeks later, I received a visa number, and they indicated that when this number was called, they had to know where to contact me so that arrangements could be made for my immigration. I mentioned that I might want to go back to Hungary first, and they said that would be all right. They reminded me that Hungary was now a Communist country and so they could not provide transportation for me to immigrate from there to the US, even though there was an American Consulate in Hungary. They advised me to return to Frankfurt, and then they would notify me about immigration arrangements when the time came. In the meantime, my friend Alter also decided to immigrate to the US.

Now I was ready to leave Frankfurt, and the American army provided transportation for me to Austria. In Vienna, I met people I knew from

Szombathely who confirmed that they had seen Tibor when they went back home. Even though Hungary was in Communist hands, Vienna was occupied by American, French, and British forces. Transportation by train was provided from Vienna and, at the Hungarian border, the officials waved me on my way and welcomed me home. I wondered how sincere that welcome was, but I tried not to think too much about it.

Hungary

The first place I stopped off was in the city of Papa. I had heard that my mother's sister, Hilda Rechnitzer was alive and living there. I found her house, andwhen she saw me, she was very happy and excited and could not stop crying. She told me that she and one of her sons had been able to get to Budapest, where they had been hidden. Her other two sons had worked in the Hungarian Army Labor Battalion. Her husband was sent to Buchenwald and never made it back. She said she did not know who was still alive, but hoped that my mother and father, with whom she had been very close, would be returning.

In the back of my mind, I had hoped that, when I returned to my city, a miracle would have happened and my parents would be there. I had also never been able to find out anything about my grandparents, who had been deported from another city. I left after the following day and told Aunt Hilda that, if I stayed in Hungary, I would visit her again soon.

I arrived on the train at Szombathely, and everything seemed strange. Almost two years had passed and the faces I saw were mostly unfamiliar ones. I took the tramway, and when I told the conductor who I was, I did not have to pay anything since I did not have any Hungarian money with me. It was Sunday morning around eleven o'clock when I appeared at Tibor's apartment. We were both surprised at the changes that had taken place. I did not look like a little boy anymore and Tibor looked older and not very well. Tears filled our eyes. I met his wife, Zsuzsi (Susie) and he said that there was room in the apartment for me and I could stay with them as long as I wished.

One day, we both went back to the house in the ghetto where we had lived before deportation. We went to the basement and dug up what father had buried. We found the copper box, but the paper money had rotted away. All our efforts under dangerous conditions had been for nothing. I decided that I wanted to see father's hardware store once again, even though Tibor told me that it had been turned into a bar. I visited the place anyway and felt very sad when I thought of the many happy times working together with father. I also went to our old apartment. Of course there were strange people living there and none of our furniture or any of our belongings were still around. I really don't know what I expected to find, but I walked away very downcast, and could not wait to leave the area. I realized that I would not find anything left of the past in Szombatheley and wished I had not returned.

I helped Tibor in his hardware store, but my heart was not in it. None of my friends and hardly any of the other people I had known had returned to the city. Only about a hundred of those who had lived there had come back. One of the few that I met was the father of my friend, Laci. When he saw me, he said, "Gyuri, did you see my son? He was in Auschwitz with you. Didn't you see him? Do you know what happened to him? I am alone now. My wife and little daughter are also gone." I had to tell him that I had not seen Laci and that I did not know what had happened to him. He began to cry, and then he screamed, "Murderers! They murdered my whole family!" There was nothing I could say to him, and I felt very sorrowful.

My best friend, Hanzi's cousin, also asked me about him. Others questioned me about my other friends. I began to feel a strong sense of guilt. Why was I alive and they were all dead? Some of the people even asked me that very question. I did not know what to answer. All this affected me deeply and, to this day, I have some unresolved feelings. Telling the story has helped.

I became acquainted with some of the younger people in Szombathely. Most of them were talking of emigrating to Palestine. There was an opportunity to go, because some of the Soviet soldiers were accepting bribes to take people overnight in their trucks to Vienna. From Vienna, transportation was arranged with the Zionist organization. I still did not want to go to Palestine or any place other than the US, although many people tried very hard to persuade me.

Months passed and I was feeling more and more unhappy. I knew that Szombathely was no longer the right place for me. I wanted to return to the American Zone, where I had felt much more comfortable. By this time, I was sure my parents had not survived, and I could not bear staying in a place where the grim memories of the recent past were all too vivid in my mind. So I spoke with Tibor about leaving. He was against it. He told me that one of our father's brothers, Uncle Bela, was alive and coming to Szombathely with his wife, Sari. After they arrived, we had long talks. He and Tibor formed a partnership in the hardware business in which I was not involved. But that was all right with me; I did not want to be part of the business. I wanted no strings to tie me to this city. I helped out and paid my way and with this arrangement, I was able to take care of myself.

The old synagogue was still in place. I went there one day and when I looked around, I did not recognize anyone. This too was depressing. Everything I did and saw in the city was like this and convinced me that since the life I had known no longer existed, I did not want to stay and try to make a new life there. I spoke with Dr. Hacker, who had opened a law practice, and he agreed that I would be making a good move to emigrate to the US to make a new start. I also spoke with Gyula Weder, father's old attorney, and he told me how much he liked and respected father and what a fine businessman he had been. He also agreed that I no longer belonged in Hungary. It was now a Communist country and everything had changed and there was no real future for me there.

During this period in Szombathely, I met an attractive Hungarian girl, and although she was not Jewish, she was very kind to me. However, there were things I did not know about her. One Sunday I went to visit her at her father's bar on the outskirts of the city. While I was having a beer, a jeep pulled up with a Soviet officer and two non-commissioned officers. They pointed at me and ordered me into the jeep, never saying another word. They drove away and, although I knew I had not done anything wrong, I was terribly afraid.

They took me to the Hungarian police station and spoke Russian to an interpreter. They told the interpreter that I had been doing black market business with the girl and that they were putting me in jail. After they left the station, the Hungarian policeman told me the real story. The girl had been dating the Soviet officer, and he did not want any interference in his relationship with her. He wanted to teach me a lesson not to have anything more to do with her, so this was just a warning, and the next morning they would probably let me out of jail.

Tibor became alarmed when he found out what had happened to me. He came to the jail the following morning, and they did let me out. For me, this experience was the last straw in my decision not to remain in Hungary. Now I made up my mind that I would leave as soon as possible.

The only pleasant experience I had on that trip to Hungary was meeting Anna, the woman who had lived with our family and helped raise my brothers and me. When I found her, she told me she had been looking all over for me. Then she took a bag out of her purse containing about a half dozen photographs of my family and myself. She had tears in her eyes when she said, "Your parents were the most wonderful people on earth, and the years I spent with your family were the happiest ever. These pictures are a treasure, and I kept hoping I would be able to give them to you, because I knew what they would mean to you." To this day, they are the only pictures I have of my family. When I told

Anna that I was planning to go to the US, she hugged me and turned around and walked away, but not before I saw tears streaming down her face.

Late in 1947, Tibor's wife, Zsuzsi, had given birth to a daughter, and it was then that he decided it was time to leave Hungary. He had accumulated some money through the business and would liquidate the store. We had to arrange our exit very carefully so that the Hungarian authorities did not become suspicious. If you were caught trying to cross the border, they would bring you back and put you in jail. We made plans for Tibor and family to leave first. I would follow in a couple of days.

Some of the local farmers who had land on both sides of the border between Hungary and Austria had been father's customers, and they thought very highly of him. When they came to Tibor's store, we told them of our plans, and they wanted to help. They told us we should set the time to leave, and they would bribe the Hungarian border guards. The Hungarian border guards were trained by the Soviet and Hungarian armies, and while the Soviets were busy with other things, they would take people across.

Shortly before all of this took place, I was in the store when Rotholz walked in. I was so amazed to see him, that I could hardly believe my eyes. He was the kapo in Dachau Allach who had told me he could not help me and had been so cruel to all the camp inmates in his charge. Now, there he was, standing before me. I became so enraged when I looked at him that I saw red. I said to Tibor, "You will see what is going to happen here now!"

Rotholz had come to sell merchandise to us, as he was once more a salesman for the Csepel factory. I could tell he did not recognize me, so, he was astonished when I leaped over the counter and grabbed him by the coat. "You filthy son of a bitch, you were a kapo in Dachau Allach. I will never forget the way you treated me and everyone else. If you don't leave this store immediately, I am going to call the police and have you arrested!" He pleaded with me not to report him, because he would lose everything. I told him, "I don't care what happens to you. Just get out of here now before I really lose my temper." He left so fast, he forgot his briefcase which I threw after him into the street. Tibor and I talked about reporting him to the Csepel factory, but then we decided to forget about Rotholz, and make our plans to leave as quickly as possible. Now Tibor was also anxious to leave Hungary.

We started at once liquidating the store, lowering prices to sell everything quickly, so that we would have money to take with us. Then, on a Sunday, Tibor and his family took an old-style taxi packed with all of their luggage and left the city, heading toward the border. A day later, the farmer who had helped them to cross the border, came to the store to tell me that Tibor was waiting for me in Vienna and asked if I was ready to go. Paul Ungar, who occasionally helped in the store planned to leave with me, because his wife had gone separately with Tibor to avoid suspicion. Ungar and I took two bicycles from the store and, around noontime, we headed for the border. Szombathely was not far from the Austrian border, and after about an hour and a half of peddling, we reached the farmer's house, where we stayed until midnight.

Exiting Hungary

The farmer told us we were ready to go when the Hungarian border guards went off in another direction. We were instructed that, when we crossed the border, we would be in Austria, and the farmer pointed to the house where we were expected; which was visible from where we stood. I thanked him, paid him, and we went across with no problem.

When we arrived at the house on the Austrian side, the farmer there told us to stay for the night. He asked us for a little money and said that he would take us to the railroad station the next morning. Once again, my ability to speak fluent German was helpful.

We arrived in Vienna where Tibor met our train. He had arranged with the Zionist organization for a place to stay. Since it was our idea to go to the US, we spent about a week in Vienna to have the best opportunity to get out. There were Soviet troops outside the city all the way to Salzburg, and so we had to find a way to get to the American sector in Germany.

We found a postmaster at the railroad station who was sending people over to the American Zone by hiding them in the baggage car of the train where the mail was stored.

We contacted him, gave him some money, and he instructed us to purchase train tickets just like any Austrian travelers would do. Before we reached the American Zone, he would signal us to come inside the postal area where he would hide us.

We boarded the train and took seats. So far, everything went smoothly. Just before we reached the American Zone where the Soviet guards came on the train to check papers, the postmaster came for us. During the trip, an Austrian lady who sat with us on the train agreed to hold my niece, Judith, on her lap. Of course, she was also paid for her help.

We reached the luggage compartment, where we were hidden , and since there was no room, we stayed in a squatting position for quite some time. We heard the Soviet soldiers walking back and forth, but they could not see us behind all the big packages. I held my breath, and we dared not make a sound. If we were caught, we would have been arrested and probably imprisoned somewhere in the Soviet Union.

The train started rolling again. After a little time, it came to a stop. We heard English being spoken and people walking through the train. We were still hiding in the luggage area and the postmaster said that we should stay there and he would come back for us when the American soldiers checked papers on the train. After about twenty minutes or so, the train started off slowly, then picked up speed. We were in the American Zone!

Tibor thanked the postmaster for his help, gave him some more money, and he brought us back to the car to rejoin Judith. Soon after we arrived at Salzburg. We received directions to a small hotel in the mountains, where we could have lodgings for the night. A taxi was called, and after riding for a while on a narrow mountain road, we arrived at a neat little hotel and made arrangements for the night. The proprietor told us that we were welcome and that we could stay as long as we wished. There was a nice large room with a big bed where Tibor and family slept, and a cot for me.

I remember the lovely down pillows and blankets. We all slept peacefully through the night, getting rid of some of the tension and fear we had experienced on the train. The next morning, we decided to stay a few more days. We went to the proprietor and asked for a small room for me; which she was able to provide, and with that arrangement, we all had our privacy. We took showers, had a good breakfast, and now we had to make a decision about what to do and where we were going. The Ungars, who had traveled with us, had a room in the same hotel. Paul Ungar told us that they were going to Paris, where he had relatives. He suggested that we go with them to Paris and assured us that his family would help us.

Tibor suggested that, since none of us had ever been to Paris, and this might be our last opportunity, we should accept Paul's offer. I was reluctant to change our plans, because I wanted to return to Germany and wait for my visa, but I agreed and we all went to Paris. I expected to stay there for a week or two and then go back to

Germany. After a few more days in that delightful mountain village. we decided to travel to Paris from Salzburg, because it was only a short distance from the German border, and it would be no problem crossing from there. When we crossed over into Germany, the German border guards asked where we were coming from. I showed them my DP card, and Tibor told them that we had escaped from the Soviets in Hungary. The German guards did not give us any problem, especially since the American MPs were also at the border.

In Munich, we were told there were trains running to the French border, which was Strasbourg, the city between France and Germany. After several hours wait, our train arrived and we were on our way.

We traveled five or six hours to Strasbourg, where we left the train and went for something to eat. We approached a taxi driver and asked him if there was any problem crossing the French border to Paris. He told us that as far as he knew, there was no problem, but to be sure, he would take us in the evening when it was most likely that there would be no patrol. The taxi was more like a mini-bus, and the driver was able to pack all our luggage in, and we started off late in the evening.

Paris

We arrived in Paris about four o'clock in the morning at the Rue du Dahomey. Paul Ungar knocked on his family's door. There was a lot of hugging and kissing, and then Paul told them that he had brought along some friends who would be staying for the day. His relatives had a very small apartment with no extra room, but they were very hospitable. We did not mind sleeping on the floor; however, we told them we would go the very next day to a Jewish organization for orientation and to see if they could help us find a place to stay.

So the next day, Paul's cousin drove Tibor and me to the Jewish organization, where we found some German-speaking people. We explained that we had just arrived in Paris and needed a place to stay. They said this was not a problem. They offered to return to the apartment with us to pick up the others and then take us to a place where the people rented to refugees.

We were driven to the Hotel du Milan in the Bastille District. The person who accompanied us from the Jewish organization told the owner of the hotel that we wanted to rent rooms and would be staying indefinitely. There was only one large room available. The price was reasonable and it came with a community bathroom. Then she gave us the news that I could not stay in the room with the others because, by law, we were too many people for the space. She gave me the address of a place where I could stay which was quite near the hotel.

We settled in and then went to a little market across the street to buy some food and other necessities; especially for Judith who was only two years old. Later in the day, I walked over to the address of the recommended hotel and found it was a three-story building with a bar on the ground floor. In very poor French, I asked for a room. They showed me a tiny room in the attic, which had only a bed, a sink and a closet. It was the only thing available. We agreed on a price and I took the room which wasn't too inviting, but I only needed it for sleeping.

Tibor and I walked around for a few days getting acquainted, and we liked what we saw and decided to stay in Paris for a little while. We went back to the Jewish organization and told them that we needed work and would take any jobs that were available. They took our names and sent someone with us to the police station to be registered. We were told we had to have papers to show if the police should stop us.

The police took down the information they needed, including some life history. They were quite sympathetic because we had escaped the Communists. We received an identification paper called a "Recepisse" which had to be renewed every six months. The police told us that we had to have this paper to register at hotels. They also told us of an Ort School that was operated by another Jewish organization where we could learn an occupation. They mentioned that the Ort School would also give us a little pocket money.

We told the Jewish organization representative who had come with us to the police station that we would return the next day. He replied that there was no need to come back unless we were not successful with the Ort School. He gave us the address, and the following day we went there.

The Ort School people told us that there were very few professions available at that time. One was running a sewing machine and another was shoemaking. Tibor decided to learn how to work a sewing machine in case, he said, we decided to do something on our own. I chose shoemaking.

My teacher in that department was a Polish Jew by the name of Monsieur Maurice who had come to France many years earlier. He had escaped deportation by hiding with French Christians during the German occupation. He was very sympathetic and told me to sit down and relax and he would explain the tools and teach me how a shoe was created step by step. At the first station in the process, I watched him cut out a model from leather. At the second station I watched others who were working on the next phase. The workers in shoemaking were a large international group—people from Hungary like myself, others from Romania and Bulgaria. A Spanish Basque among them had been permitted to come into the Ort School, and because he already knew the operation, he was second in charge. Spanish was his only language (other than his native Basque) and although we could not really converse, we used hand gestures to convey our meaning. In this way, we communicated quite well. I remember that he always had a nice and friendly smile.

Tibor and I had a little savings left from the money we brought out of Hungary, and we received some additional pocket money from the Ort School. But, what we had was not enough to live on and we had to earn more.

Tibor had made friends with a Hungarian from Budapest whose name was Laci. He was a very pleasant person who occasionally invited us to his apartment for dinner. Tibor's wife had started to do some cooking, but since she had only an electric hot plate available in their hotel room, she was limited. We had purchased some utensils and set up for light housekeeping and I took all my meals with them.

Life in Paris was not easy in the beginning. We had to become accustomed to different ways of doing things and the strangeness of our surroundings plus trying to learn the French language. In addition, when I went to that attic room to sleep, the noise from the bar below sometimes kept me awake. I began to have flashbacks and nightmares about my parents and my brother Izidor. Some nights I could not stop thinking of the things that had happened to all of us. During those hours, that little room would close in on me. I felt overwhelmed by my circumstances. Then I would tell myself that, if I could survive those terrible times in the camps, I could certainly get through this time and overcome these dark thoughts of the recent past. Although my life was nothing like what I would have foreseen, I knew that I could endure it.

I am sure the strength I always found when I needed it most came from my upbringing and the secure and loving childhood my parents had given me. Growing up, I had always felt very much loved by my family, and this love gave me a feeling of security in the worst of times. No matter how they tried to make us feel less-than-human in the camps, nothing they did could erase the warm and beautiful memories of my early years; especially memories of my mother who had loved and enjoyed life to the fullest.

Now in Paris, I reasoned that I was very young, and my life was no longer threatened. I had my health and, although Paris was strange to me, I would get used to everything. People were helping us and conditions would improve. With such thoughts to comfort me, I found myself gradually coming out of that awful depression.

Learning to make shoes, I made a lot of mistakes. I was shown how to cut certain models out of the leather, but the first time I tried it on my own, I used the back side instead of the surface, and the models all came out opposite the way they were supposed to be. The other workers laughed at me and the backward models I had so laboriously done were all thrown out. Monsieur Maurice patiently showed me how to do it right.

Tibor's wife remembered that, on her father's side, there were some relatives named Roder who went to Paris before the war. We went to the Jewish organization and they assured us that, if these people lived in Paris, they would find them. Two weeks later, someone came to our hotel from the organization to tell us the news that they were sure they had found the

Roder family. These people were successful manufacturers of ladies garments and appeared to be quite wealthy.

Zsuzsi telephoned them, but she could not speak a word of French. So she asked if they spoke Hungarian and they immediately understood and answered her. Then she knew for sure that they were her father's relatives. They were very pleased to hear from her.

This first contact with the Roders occurred on a weekday, and so they arranged to pick us up on the following Sunday. They took us to their home for the day. Other relatives had also gathered there to meet us, and we had what felt like a family reunion; strangers though we were. A delicious dinner was served, and we all enjoyed a conversation in Hungarian.

Everyone there told us that Paris was a very beautiful city and that the French would treat us very well, especially after what had happened to us. They suggested that we learn the language as quickly as possible in order to feel more at home. They also suggested that we settle down and stay for a while because they felt we could have a very nice life there. Even though Tibor and I expected our stay to be brief, it turned out that we were in Paris for about two years.

The Roders offered Tibor some money, which he tried to decline, but they were insistent. They also told us that they would ask their acquaintances to try to find us good jobs. They said that any time we needed help, we should call upon them and they would do whatever they could for us. Those words gave us a good feeling to know that, if necessary, we could count on a family who were concerned about us. After that first visit, we saw the Roders quite often, and they showed us around Paris. We visited Notre Dame, the Rue de Rivoli and many other famous sights. We went with them on a boat ride on the Seine River and enjoyed some excellent restaurants. We had some good times with that wonderful family, but most of all, we had people who cared about us in this strange city.

One evening, Tibor and I were walking on the street when, in front of a candy store, I noticed a man I thought I recognized, even though his back was turned toward me. I approached him and saw that it was the Frenchman Jacques with whom I had worked at the BMW factory. I still could not speak very much French, so I said in German, "Dachau Allach—BMW." He stared at me looking very shocked and replied in a combination of Yiddish and German and blurted out, "It is you, It is really you. I remember we worked together. But how did you recognize me?" I told him that once I see a face, I never forget. We hugged each other, and both of us were delighted to meet again.

Jacques took us into the candy store where he bought us all kinds of treats. Then he invited us to his home and we became good friends. Jacques had a position in City Hall, and he said that he would be more than happy to do whatever he could to give us a helping hand. Fortunately, it was not necessary to take advantage of his generous offer just then. When you go through such an experience as we did at Dachau Allach, you not only become friends, but a special bond develops between you. I thought, what a wonderful coincidence that Jacques and I should meet this way on a Paris street.

Although at the time, the economy of Paris was not good and most food was still rationed, we went to the area of St. Paul, a Jewish district, where there was a huge delicatessen. We always could pick up some additional food items there.

A few weeks later, the Roder family told me that an acquaintance of theirs was looking for a young person to work in their pajama factory and that I should go and meet with him. They told Tibor that something might also be coming up for him soon too. We had learned the metropolitan subway system and so I was able to go from Tibor's hotel directly to the factory. The metro system had not been difficult to learn. There were push-buttons for every direction you would want to go and with a map, it was easy.

Since I could not speak fluent French, the man whom I was to see spoke to me in Yiddish, and some of what he said I understood because of the similarity to German. He told me he was born in Poland and had come to France years before. He said he was lucky he could hide in Paris during the war and now he had a business. He said he was looking for someone to replace an employee who was leaving. The job was cutting out pajama pieces for assembly by jobbers and he would train me himself. We talked awhile, and he seemed to like me and said that he hoped I would qualify.

He took me to a big table and showed me how to lay out the pajama material and put the models down. He had a big cutting machine for the job and warned me to be very careful or I could lose a finger, even though there was a safety mechanism around the blade. I learned the operation quickly, because I was eager to earn some money. After a few days, I could cut the patterns myself. He was extremely kind and said he wanted me to meet his family. So now things began to look a bit brighter. I was shown where I would work in a big attic that had many windows and was breezy and bright. My boss's name was George Katzman and I called him Monsieur George. He would give me instructions in the morning as to how many of each size pajama to cut and on which material.

After four or five days, the job became quite easy. I learned that certain women would come to pick up the work which they would then complete. I had to count carefully what I gave them, because the following week they would bring back the ready-made pajamas. Sometimes they had to wait until I finished cutting the material. They were mostly older women, but one day an attractive lady in her early thirties came in. She introduced herself as Lillian and she told me she came from Belgium. I noticed that, while she waited for her bundle, she always stared at me and smiled. I smiled back. One day, she came very nicely dressed and walked over to where I was working and kissed me. I was quite surprised, but then she told me that she was a widow and had no man in her life for quite some time. She hinted that she would like to be friends with me, and at that point in my life, the suggestion sounded appealing. One day the following week, she appeared in my attic shop, at once locked the door and began to undress. After I recovered from the momentary shock, I got the message, and we began a rather enjoyable relationship.

There was also among the women who came to pick up their pajama work, a younger woman who introduced herself as Tema from Russia. She told me she lived with her parents and a sister. She asked if I could give her extra work, because the family needed the money badly. I was able to arrange to do so, and she was very grateful. Tema was very pretty, but I did not approach her for fear of jeopardizing my job. Meantime, Lillian was visiting me several times a week, always at the same time. We had to be very discreet.

As time went on, Tema became more and more talkative and asked a lot of questions about my past. Once she invited me to the movies with her—the Rex, the largest theater in Paris. They were playing "Captain from Castille" with Tyrone Power. I accepted and went to her house by metro to pick her up. We saw the movie, then went to a nearby cafe for coffee and dessert—and talked for a long time.

We became very good friends, and although we occasionally kissed, nothing beyond that developed. She told me she also intended to go to the US and perhaps we would meet there again. We agreed that we should remain just friends as long as we were in Paris. For my part, I really needed this kind of companionship, as I was still dealing with the pain from the loss of my parents and Izidor.

Unfortunately, my other brother Tibor and I had never been close, even growing up. He had not been close with anyone in the family. Most of the time, he did what he wanted to do, regardless of what our parents said, and they were often very upset by his behavior. Tibor stuttered as a child, but no one seemed to realize at that time that the stutter might indicate an emotional problem, so he was just considered a disobedient child. Tibor and I thought very differently about many things, and he was always convinced that his way was the only right way. During our Paris days, I often thought how sad it was that we did not have a good relationship, since we were the only ones left from our immediate family.

One day at work, I brought some pajama material down to the retail store for someone. Monsieur George's wife, Madame Katzman, was there. She came over to me and said, "I haven't had the opportunity to speak with you, so when you finish your work today, why don't you come down and I will take you to lunch."

At the restaurant, while we were waiting for our food, she told me that for both Monsieur George and herself, this was a second marriage. She told me that they both had daughters from their previous marriages. She said that her daughter was about my age, and asked if I would like to take her to a movie one day. I had seen her daughter, and I was not very interested, but I did not want to offend Madame Katzman. I replied that, while I found her daughter attractive, I was seeing a girl called Tema, and I did not want to hurt her. She told me that she knew the Russian girl and thought her nice and very pretty. She said she understood my feelings.

I did eventually date her daughter a couple of times, but my heart always pulled toward Tema. Meanwhile, Tema took me to her father's kosher restaurant in the St. Paul district, and she introduced me to her mother and sister. As time went on, we became even closer friends.

During our first year in Paris, 1948, Tibor registered with the American Consulate. The officials there told him that the visa process would take about a year and that he must be patient. He also had taken a job with another manufacturer that had been arranged through the Roder family. So, between the two of us, we were earning good money. These earnings enabled us to do more in Paris and we visited most of the places worth seeing plus attending quite a few soccer matches. Almost every weekend, Tibor and his family and I went to a different park. The parks in Paris were beautifully manicured and we all enjoyed these outings. To this day, they are known to be among the loveliest parks in the world.

In 1948, the economy started improving in France. No one needed a ration card any longer, and very soon almost everything became available. We were fortunate in that someone told us about an apartment near the Eiffel tower district that we might be able to rent. We went to look at it and found that the people who lived in other apartments there were also refugees. They told us that the rent would not be any more than we were already paying for our two separate rooms. The apartment was quite small, but I would have a room of my own. Tibor and his family would have their room, and it had a small kitchen. We all liked the place and decided to take it. So I finally could move out of that dismal attic room.

In May, 1949, Tibor was called to the American Consulate. They told him that everything checked out and that he could emigrate to the US. I also went to the Consulate and was advised to return to Munich and request that my papers be transferred from Frankfurt. I was told that my number would be coming up soon.

In June, 1949, Tibor and his family left for the US. Since I was alone in the apartment, I invited Laci, Tibor's Hungarian acquaintance to share the apartment with me, which he did.

Now I had to make a decision as to what I wanted to do because, although life had become very good in Paris, if I wanted to go to the US, I had to go back to Germany and wait there for my visa. I stayed in Paris for another month, during which time I visited the Roder family to tell them I was preparing to return to Germany. They tried to persuade me to stay, but I told them it was my lifelong dream to go to the US, and that I would go as soon as my visa was issued. I said my good-byes to the Roders and then went to Monsieur George.

I was sad to leave him, because my job had worked out so well in every respect. He also tried to persuade me not to leave. When he realized that I would not change my mind, he asked me to keep in touch because he considered me family. I volunteered to find someone to take my place. I went to the Jewish organization, and they recommended a fellow about my age whom I then showed how to do the job. At least I was not leaving Monsieur George stranded. I also said good-bye to my Belgian friend Lillian.

Then came the worst part - saying good-bye to Tema. She cried and said, "I know we will meet in America, since my family is also planning to go to New York." I gave Tema my uncle's address, and then we parted.

I gave up the apartment to someone who was happy to get it since, at that time, apartments were very scarce in Paris. Laci and I left together. I was heartbroken, because

I had to leave so many friends, including Jacques who made me promise to keep in touch. Leaving Paris was very difficult because it had begun to feel like home. Once again, I had to break up everything and go to still another strange place where I did not know what the future would hold. In spite of the pain, I made the break because the dream was so compelling for me. I was determined to go to the US, even if I had to start out there digging ditches.

It was the end of July 1944, when Laci and I took an overnight train to Munich. When we crossed over the French-German border, we showed our French ID cards and they asked us why we were going to Munich. When we told them we were going to emigrate to the US, they sent us on our way. The reason we chose Munich was that Immigration had told us the city had become a center for emigration and would be the easiest and best place to get help. The American Consulate in Paris had given us similar advice.

Munich

The train arrived at the Munich railroad station at seven o'clock in the morning August 1, 1949. We went to a nearby coffee shop and then asked directions from a policeman to the local Jewish organization. When we arrived, we were given papers to fill out, and we became members of that organization. They told us that they would do whatever they could to assist us. They suggested that as long as we were there, we should go back to the Ort School, which we did. I told the people at Ort of my experience at the Ort School in Paris in shoemaking. They said there was no shoemaking department at this school. Instead, they offered me other leather products, such as luggage and purses. Laci went to a department where he could use a sewing machine to make shirts, which is what he had done in Paris.

The Ort School in Munich had a small community building with free rooms, but unfortunately that facility was full. So we were sent to the Schwabing district, an artist colony, where we could find accommodations in a panzion, which was a hotel for students and cost very little money. We took the tramway to what turned out to be large attractive building. There we rented a room. The panzion was a very pleasant place with a lovely view overlooking grass and trees. We settled in and were quite comfortable.

The next day, I went to the American Consulate and showed them my papers from the consulate in Frankfurt. They told me the number I had was the number I would need to emigrate. Once the papers were transferred, they might need me to come in to answer further questions.

At the Ort School in Munich, I met a lot of people, some of whom I had known at the Paris school. Some were in Munich to emigrate to the US; others were there to emigrate to Canada and a few were going to Brazil.

I did not know Tibor's address in New York, so I wrote to him in care of our uncle, who forwarded the letter to him. I also corresponded with Monsieur George in Paris and with Tema. I told her that, when she came to America, she could probably find me either through the Jewish organization or even in the telephone book under my uncle's name.

I was feeling pretty good. I had enough money saved and occasionally Tibor sent me a few dollars. I did not need much—just for food and rent, which was not expensive, and I had enough clothing. So things in Munich went smoothly for me, and I kept myself busy.

Munich had been bombed continuously during the war, and I remember seeing the fires from far away when I was in the camps. Thanks to the Marshall Plan, the city had been rebuilt and was beautiful once again.

At that time, Germany's post-war president, Konrad Adenauer, announced that any one of us Jews who wanted to settle in Germany would be given German citizenship. He also pledged loans if any of us wanted to go back to school. Some people did decide to settle in Germany, but the prospect did not entice me. Munich was too close to Dachau Allach, and I had the feeling that, although the Germans made these offers, Jewish citizens were not really desired in

Germany. I did not wish to remain any longer than necessary.

I met a few nice people in our building with whom I started to become friendly, but then Laci and I found another panzion on the outskirts of Munich, which had a large room and a community bathroom for less money than we had been paying, so we decided to move there.

When we were not busy at the Ort School, we visited coffee houses, went to the movies and often did sightseeing around Munich. One Saturday evening, Laci and I were in the Café Leopold. The waiter brought me a glass of whiskey and pointed out a woman at another table. He told me that the lady had sent over the drink and wished to make my acquaintance. I walked over to where she was seated, and she invited me to sit down. She was very well dressed and quite attractive, and introduced herself as Ilke. She explained, "I watched you for a while, and you remind me of someone I know. So I wanted to meet you, since you look so familiar." I did not know at that time that her line was a variation of, "Haven't we met somewhere before?" I told her my background—who I was, where I came from. When I came to the part about the camps, she was shocked and said she had heard about the Dachau concentration camp. She expressed great compassion. Then she said, "I am German, but it certainly doesn't matter to me that you are Jewish, and I would really like us to be friends."

She invited me to her apartment, which was beautifully furnished. Looking around, I noticed a picture of a soldier in a Wehrmacht uniform. She hastened to apologize for leaving the photograph out. It was a picture of her husband who had been killed on the Russian front. She put the photograph away. We talked and had a few drinks and spent a pleasant evening.

She told me she owned a very fine store in the city which handled art and antiques. If I wished, I could come and help her there in the daytime. I declined because I did not want to leave the Ort School or my friends. Ours turned out to be an enjoyable friendship; she was good company for the couple of months I had left in Munich.

Shortly, I received word from the American Consulate requesting that I report and fill out some forms. I was told that I would be questioned again and that my papers were being processed. The questioning was done at a little building occupied by the American Counterintelligence Corps. They had interpreters on the staff, and although they were friendly, the questioning was extensive. This was, after all, in late 1949 when there was grave concern in America about Communist affiliations. I told them that the only organization I had belonged to was the Jewish Federation, and I showed them the membership card. When they were finished questioning me, they said I would hear from them fairly soon regarding my emigration.

From October on, the holiday season in Germany was very festive. The season is called Fasching and people everywhere were celebrating, particularly since the economy had improved. The weather was turning cold, but I had an overcoat I had brought from Paris. Our crowd still went to the Café Leopold most Saturday nights, and so we celebrated the Christmas holidays there. In the Ort School, they gave a Chanukah party. In spite of all the festivities I was becoming impatient to hear when I could leave the country.

Tibor and my uncle both answered my letters. My uncle wrote reassuring me that, when I came to the US, everything would be taken care of. I would be able to go to school, if that is what I chose to do. He wrote how much he was looking forward to seeing me. He mentioned over and over again how close he and my mother had been, and he recalled fond memories of when they were young. He commented that I was lucky to have survived all the terrible things that had happened, and repeated that he could not wait until I arrived in New York. His letters meant a lot to me and I really looked forwarding to seeing him.

I kept going to the Ort School and made some new friends. One was from Romania and another from Czechoslovakia. We went out together and always had a good time. One Saturday evening, I happened to meet a very attractive German lady named Monica, who told me right off that she was married and had two children. She said that her relationship with her husband was not a good one and that they went their separate ways, even though they both lived in their home with their children.

I told her that if she wanted me as a friend that was fine, but I did not want any problems with her husband. She assured me that this would not be an issue, since he was out of town most of the time, and they really did lead separate lives. I told her I went to school every day, but she said she had free time in the afternoons and would like to visit me then. She came to my place two or three time a week. On a few Sundays, we went together with her children to a swimming pool. I enjoyed her company, as she was interesting to talk to and fun to be with. But, I did explain to her that I was waiting to leave Munich and would not be staying a moment longer than necessary. She replied that if she were in my place, she would do the same thing.

It took longer than I had anticipated because it wasn't until July 1950, that I was notified by the American authorities that I should report in early August to the Funkasserne, which was the German barracks for the army. They gave me the date and a number, and said I would be processed to go to the US. I was very excited to hear this news, and immediately started to get ready and pack my things. When I reported, I was interviewed again and examined physically; including my teeth. Then they told me I had passed everything, and should report to Bremerhaven with all of my belongings as soon as I was notified of the exact date. A week later, the letter came with the date of August 10th. I bade good-bye to all my friends, and in the meantime, Laci had applied for a visa with the Canadian government. That was where he was going, so we talked about meeting again in New York or perhaps in Canada.

I took the train to Bremerhaven, and there the MPs called out names from a long list. As I started up the ramp to the ship, I became so excited that I could not catch my breath. At long last, the moment I had been dreaming about and waiting for was happening. I was on my way to

America! As we arrived on deck, they handed all the men a bucket of paint and a brush. A German interpreter explained that this was an army troop ship that had brought soldiers over to Europe during the war. Since the ship was now rusty, they were asking us to paint it instead of charging any fare. I was so happy that I didn't care what I had to do to cross that ocean.

Voyage to America

The ship, the General Langfitt, was very crowded so we slept way below decks. Men and women were in separate areas. We painted a bit for a few hours, took a break and tried to hold conversations with the sailors.

At night, we went to the top deck where they played music. I always looked around to see if I could find anyone I knew, but the ship was very crowded and I had no success. As soon as we reached the English Channel, I became terribly sick and that awful feeling would not go away. This was my first ocean voyage; therefore my first experience with sea sickness. I was given Dramamine, but it did not help. They told me there was nothing else that could be done. They said I must force myself to eat something, because if I didn't, the nausea would get worse.

When the ocean calmed, I was able to eat and drink a little, but as soon as the sea became choppy and the boat started rocking, I was in bad shape. Finally, it was so bad, I had to tell them I could not paint anymore because the paint fumes were making me feel worse. There were a lot of seasick people on the ship, and they advised us to stay on the top deck where the motion was not so strong.

Movies from the US were shown, and one that I will always remember was the life of George M. Cohan. I particularly liked the song, "Give My Regards to Broadway". It sounded so "American" to me.

We were given instructions in German. They explained the money exchange, and gave examples of the prices of various items. They also showed us pictures of New York City, and gave lectures in which they tried to provide us with some idea of what to expect in our new country. We were warned not to become frustrated if we did not get jobs right away. They said there were a lot of religious organizations in all denominations that were ready to help us. Also, they made a point that we should consider investigating schools and learn the English language as quickly as we could. All this information helped a great deal to give us some idea of what to look forward to.

After almost three weeks into the journey, we arrived at New Orleans, where about 500 people left the ship. When we docked, and the motion of the ship had ceased, I soon felt much better. We stayed on deck all day while people departed, and the ship took on provisions.

The next day, they told us we were on the Mississippi River and that, although we would be on the open sea soon again, the waters would be calm for the most part, and we should not be concerned about getting seasick.

As we approached New York a few days later, announcements were made that we should watch for the lady in the harbor with a crown on her head and her hands reaching out. It was the famous Statue of Liberty. The next morning after breakfast, the captain announced that we should go on deck, because the statue of the lady would be coming up shortly. When we passed her, most everyone was filled with great emotion; some people cried with happiness, hardly believing that at last we had reached our destination.

We saw the large skyscrapers of Manhattan, and I could not believe my eyes. I marveled that these buildings did not fall over at that great height. We even saw the busy traffic from far away, and we were astounded by all of the hustle and bustle that was taking place. As the ship came closer to the docks, we were handed a form containing about a hundred questions, many of them requiring only a "yes" or "no" answer regarding membership in various organizations. Once again, this type of query was no problem for me. They collected the papers and told us to get ready and that before we left the ship an immigration inspector would look at the papers in case there were any further questions.

Finally the ship docked, and I saw Red Cross ladies sitting at tables with coffee and platters of donuts. The delicious aroma of the coffee overcame the obnoxious diesel smell, and I became very anxious to get off the ship and finally be on American soil. My head was whirling with thoughts that my dream was about to come true. Almost every night on the ship, I would wonder about whom I would eventually marry, what kind of family I would have, and always in my dreams, my wife would be the most beautiful and wonderful woman imaginable.

As we started down the gangplank, the immigration inspector took our papers. Our names were on a little card which he compared with the forms we had turned in earlier. When he stopped me, I became alarmed; however, he explained that there was one place on the form that I had not signed. I asked what it meant, and he explained with a smile that, since I was so young, Uncle Sam might want me to serve in the armed forces. The signature they required was my agreement to serve if called. Of course, I signed right away. Then the inspector said, "Welcome to the United States of America. You are now on your own."

New York

I knew that everyday, the New York papers reported which ships would be arriving, so I expected Tibor to be waiting for me. Sure enough, as I went down the gangplank, I spotted my brother. I heard him call out, "Here I am! Here I am!"

People were wandering around and some were screaming (this time the screams were screams of joy). There was confusion and a great deal of noise coming from every direction. I could not believe that I was finally on American soil. I looked around me and suddenly I felt overcome with emotion. Nothing seemed real, but then the taste of my first American donut and coffee was simply wonderful, and it helped to restore some feeling of tranquility.

As we walked away, Tibor told me the first thing I needed was a haircut, so we went to a barbershop. The barber suggested that I have a shave at the same time. Tibor tried to talk me out of it, because in the Orthodox Jewish religion, you are not allowed to use a razor blade, only an electric shaver. However, much to Tibor's annoyance, I told the barber to go ahead and give me a shave. The next thing I knew, the barber flipped the chair without warning so that I would be in a flat position. I let out a howl, because I thought I would fly out and hit the roof. I was not accustomed to this kind of automatic barber's chair. This was a new experience for me.

From the barbershop, we took a cab to Tibor's apartment. On the way, he gave me the unexpected and shocking news that Uncle Harry had suffered a heart attack and died just about the time I had left Munich. I could not believe this had happened. I felt as though my heart sank down to my shoes as I wondered what would become of me now in this utterly strange country. I had looked forward to meeting and living with my uncle, and now this would never happen. Tibor said that Uncle Harry's children had left New York for California soon after his death, so I would not have a chance to meet them either. This news was a terrible setback in the start of my new life in the US.

The apartment in which Tibor and his family lived was so small that there was no place for me to sleep there and I would have to go elsewhere. He thought he had written to me that his wife had given birth to another daughter five months earlier, but this was the first time I heard that news. After we had something to eat, Tibor took me by subway to the office of a relative whose name was Otto Schiff He was a distant older cousin of my mother's from Vienna. When we arrived at Uncle Otto's office, he welcomed me and said that he had arranged for me to sleep at his next door neighbor's apartment, since his apartment was also too small to accommodate another person. I began to feel a little uncomfortable.

It was late afternoon and Tibor left. Uncle Otto, who helped with immigration papers for a Jewish organization called Agudath Israel of America, told me to wait while he finished what he was doing. I was unable to read the magazines and newspapers there because they were all in English, so I looked out of the window and watched people in the street. Everyone seemed to be rushing somewhere.

There was so much traffic and activity going on that I just watched it all in amazement.

When Uncle Otto was ready, we went to his apartment, which was at 839 West End Avenue. I was very tired from all the excitement of the day and so, shortly after dinner, we went to his neighbor's apartment. The people there were all sitting around the living room which was beautifully furnished and very elegant. Although they were reasonably polite to me, they were rather formal and cool, and I did not feel too comfortable. I was shown to a bedroom where I fell on the bed exhausted. However, as tired as I was, I could not fall asleep. The night sounds, especiallly the traffic seemed especially loud. After a very restless night, I awoke the following morning and soon after Uncle Otto came for me. We went to his office and Tibor picked me up there. We took the subway to our cousin Ili's apartment. She was the cousin whom I had visited in Eschwege, at the big house where she lived with all those other girls. Now she had two children and a large apartment. She invited me to stay for the night, and as long as necessary.

The following morning, I accompanied Tibor to the quilting factory where he worked. They were always looking for people to work because they had a day and night shift. The owners of the factory had been fortunate to have left Vienna before Hitler took over. They came to the US and opened this factory with fifteen to twenty machines. They told me that, if I decided to work there, I should stay for the day and just observe. They explained that, in order to work in America, I must apply for a social security card. The process would take about two weeks, but since they needed help, they would allow me to start work the next day.

I watched the operations all that day. I was not happy when I heard one of the owners refer to some of the employees as "those refugees" in a derogatory way. Most of the employees were wither Puerto Ricans or Americans. That attitude did not sit well with me, because I thought that he was deliberately demeaning all of us. Nevertheless, I was determined to take the job and make the best of it.

The next morning, Tibor gave me an old pair of khaki pants. I started working slowly on the machine to which I was assigned. There were eighty to one hundred needles going back and forth at a rapid pace, and I had been warned not to get my fingers caught. I was shown how to feed the material into the machine, and I picked it up very quickly.

The wage was 75¢ an hour. I worked from eight in the morning until six or seven in the evening. With overtime, I earned $70 to $80 a week, which was considered quite good money at that time. I did not need too much for living costs, and so I started to save some. I asked to work even longer hours and they told me the only way was to work the night shift, which I volunteered to do. This arrangement did not work out too well. The second night, I dozed off for a few seconds and one of the needles went through one of my fingers. They took me to a nearby hospital emergency room where a doctor tended the wound and said I could return to work the next day. The owner's son was sent to check on what had happened, but I told him that I was fine and decided to remain on the night shift for a while. I had learned a lesson and never fell asleep on the job again.

Eventually, I changed back to working days, so that I could study at night. I began to read and to learn about the customs and culture in the US and tried to improve my English. I was undecided as to whether I should continue working or go back to school full time. I was now living with Tibor and his family who had moved to Brownsville in Brooklyn where many immigrants lived. The neighborhood was not too bad in those years, and it was what we could afford. I contributed to the household in this arrangement, which benefited all of us.

One day we received a call from my mother's niece Lisa who had immigrated to Canada. She was the sister of my very good friend Ervin whom I mentioned previously, as being as close to me as a brother and the news she had for us was very bad. Someone from the city of Sopron survived Auschwitz and told her that Ervin had been forced to remove the gold teeth from the dead bodies of prisoners, and he became infected and died. Another sorrowful ending, of yet another young life.

This period was not a happy time in my life. Things were not turning out as I had expected.

The death of my uncle had meant a complete change in my introduction to life in the US. I had been looking forward to being part of his household where I would have had someone who cared about me and would help me to make my new life. The few relatives we had did not seem at all interested in us. In fact they often acted as though our experiences in the ghetto and the camps were an embarrassment to them. New acquaintances made it clear that the subject of the Holocaust was one that made them uncomfortable and they did not wish to know anything about that time. I imagine that due to the reception we received, many of us stopped speaking about those times, which resulted in the bottling up our feelings for many years to come. On top of this, my relationship with my brother had not improved over the years. I began to feel very sorry that I had left Paris where I had begun to feel at home, had made so many friends, and altogether, my life had been a much happier one.

We had a distant cousin whose name was Emmi Goldschmidt. I remember that she and her sister Anni used to come to our house in Hungary very often, because their mother (my mother's sister) had died at an early age. Later, Emmi moved to Berlin, where she married and her husband owned a department store. When Hitler came to power, they emigrated to the US from Berlin. I visited her in New York occasionally, and she tried to persuade me to go back to school. I wanted very much to do just that, but I had to have money to support myself. Taking Emmi's advice into account, I decided to keep on working at the quilting factory and go to night school.

Tibor's second daughter, Kathryn suddenly became very ill. None of the doctors were able to give an accurate diagnosis. Every month she had to go to Kings County Hospital in Brooklyn because of congested lungs and an alarmingly poor appetite. Regardless of the care and medication that she received, Kathryn's condition kept worsening. The doctors at Kings County Hospital referred her case to Presbyterian Medical Center for further tests and she had to go there every two to three months for observation. Eventually, she was diagnosed with Cystic Fibrosis, an inherited disease involving the pancreas. Years later, when I returned from service in the US army, I found out that Kathryn was extremely sick and had been hospitalized. There was no known cure for the disease, and most children who were afflicted did not live into their teens. Sadly, Kathryn died at age thirteen.

The quilting factory where I worked was expanding during that post-war period. Within a year of taking the job, I received a raise to one dollar an hour. One day, the owner announced he was going to do something "nice" for the employees, especially, he said, "for the refugees." I resented these remarks and was sure that, sooner or later, I would speak out, because his attitude annoyed me so much. Then the owner said that he was going to purchase a refrigerator for us to keep our lunches in, since almost everyone "brown-bagged" it. The following week, a dilapidated old machine with the motor on top appeared in the workers' lunch area. It looked like something left over from the previous century. When the motor started, the whole machine shook and made a loud noise, but mainly, it did not keep anything cold. In Europe, I had seen refrigerators copied from US models, and they were nothing like this shabby old machine.

A few days went by and my annoyance toward the owner got the best of me. I took a piece of cardboard and printed on it in black ink, "Please take this so-called refrigerator back to Noah's Ark where it belongs" and taped it to the door of the machine. Some of the other workers asked me why I did this because they were afraid to get into trouble. I said, "When he brags about doing something "nice" and expects us to be grateful, it really should be something nice, and I think this so-called gift is an insult."

Later in the afternoon, the owner noticed the note and became very angry. He called us all together and told us that he was trying hard to be good to us. He said he meant well and did not deserve such treatment. Then he asked who put up the note. I stepped forward and said, "I did. You always refer to us as 'those refugees', and I resent that. We are new immigrants, the same as you were when you came to this country. This old machine is an insult, and you expect us to be grateful. I would never put my lunch in there." He turned to me angrily and said, "You're fired." Probably that was what I wanted to happen because I was not at all unhappy about it. I asked him when I could pick up my paycheck and he told me to come by on Friday.

I looked around the city and soon found a similar factory. I was hired immediately, and it turned out to be a much nicer place to work and closer to where I lived. I was allowed to work overtime from the beginning, and so I knew I had made a good move. At the time, my English was not good enough and I was still going to night school; however, I was still undecided as what I wanted to do with my future.

I had made a few acquaintances, but the person I liked best was Michael Rosenfeld, who lived not very far from me. Having lost all of my good childhood friends and again lost all the friends I had made through all the different moves, I found it difficult to form close relationships. I'm sure it was the fear of once again losing someone I cared for.

Tibor was following Orthodox rules rather strictly, and, of course, I respected his wishes in the home. But I felt far removed from that way of life, and I was feeling increasingly uncomfortable with it. Sometimes on Saturdays, which is the Jewish Sabbath, Mike and I would take the subway into Manhattan and spend the day doing all kinds of things. One of the Orthodox rules is that you cannot ride anywhere on the Sabbath. I never discussed any of this with Tibor and I did not know if he knew or suspected where I went or what I did, but I thought I was old enough to run my own life. Once in a while, I went with him to synagogue on a Saturday, but as I had very little in common with the people that he hung around with, being in their company only made me, and them ill at ease.

One day in 1951, about a year after I arrived in New York, Tibor was hired at a new quilting factory opening up near the line between New York City and New Jersey. Because he was so knowledgeable about machinery, they appointed him to oversee the work. They told him they were looking for more people; therefore, Tibor suggested they hire me, and they were agreeable, especially since I now had experience. The commute was longer, but the new factory was clean and very nice, and the people who ran it were very pleasant and all the employees were treated very well. Everyone was friendly, and in the mornings, we stopped for coffee and donuts and at lunch, we were given enough time to go out.

Now that I was making steady money, I bought my first suit and started to build up a nice wardrobe. As more time went by, I met and dated several American girls, and some who had also immigrated to the US. One of my dates was a very attractive girl from New Rochelle whom I liked, but she demanded a commitment, which I was nowhere near ready to give at that time.

One Saturday night, Mike and I went on a double date with two young Hungarian women. From the start, they behaved in a snobbish manner and acted as though they were doing us a favor by going out with us. We had made plans to take them to Radio City Music Hall, which, at that time, had a stage show and a movie and then we were going out to eat. We went ahead with our plans in spite of their unpleasant behavior, which did not improve as the evening progressed.

After the show, we went to have a bite to eat and as we were getting ready to leave the restaurant, to our surprise, our dates insisted that we take them home by cab—from Manhattan to Brooklyn! Such a cab trip would have been very expensive, and this demand was the last straw. I excused myself to go to the men's room and motioned to Mike to go with me so that we could discuss what to do. I said, "I've had enough of these girls and their attitude. I'm not the kind of person who would normally do such a thing, but I think we should just leave them at the table and let them get home on their own." Mike agreed, and we never went back to the table. We hoped that they learned a good lesson, but I doubt that they did. They had us pegged as greenhorns and thought they could take advantage, but they went too far.

One day in 1952, in my second year in New York, I received a postcard from the Draft Board, US Army Headquarters, New York. The card directed me to report the following week. The notice reminded me of the paper I had signed two years previously as I was preparing to leave the troop ship in New York harbor that had brought us to America from Bremerhaven. I was about to be inducted into the Armed Services of the United States of America!

I was happy to be required to serve in appreciation of what the US Army had done for the camp survivors back in 1945. Not only had they liberated us, but they had restored our dignity by the manner in which they treated us. I could not have been more proud than to have become a part of that army.

When I arrived at the induction station a week later, the first step in the process was a physical checkup, then an examination by a psychiatrist who asked me a lot of personal questions about my past and what I was doing now. Then an announcement was made that everyone in the room had qualified, and we were about to be inducted into the US Army. I was delighted. We were asked to raise our right hands and swear allegiance to the Constitution of the United States. Then they told us to return to our homes and report on a particular day the following week to Camp Kilmer, New Jersey. We were to bring only the clothes we wore, toothbrush, tooth paste, and very little money. They explained that we would be given "the flying twenty" when we arrived at Kilmer. That was the up-front pocket money for necessities before our first payday.

I went directly home and told Tibor I had been inducted into the US Army. He was not happy, because the turn of events did not coincide with the plans we had made to go into some kind of business together. He had an idea about selling baby blankets, which he had already started working on, and now he would have to take someone else into the business. He asked me to come up with a name for the company and I offered the name, "Stork Baby Blankets", which he accepted. I also suggested that when he went into the stores to sell the blankets, that each one should be in a box the same color as the blanket—either blue. pink, white or yellow. That idea would cost a little extra money, but it would be novel and eye catching. He really liked the idea, and later I found out that he used all my suggestions in the business.

I was not at all satisfied with my life in New York and was actually looking forward to a change; even such a drastic one.

Service in the U.S. Army

I was inducted into the United States Army in December, 1952. The Korean Conflict was just coming to an end. The first day at Camp Kilmer we received a general briefing, and were told that we would be there for a one-week orientation. We were issued uniforms and directed to mail home all our civilian clothes. We received shots, took showers and put on our new uniforms. They issued us six pairs of socks and underwear, a dress uniform and fatigues. All these, except what we put on, went into a duffel bag.

The discipline was laid on from the very start. We were required to move double-time from one place to another. Our sergeant made his voice heard "loud and clear ", which was the army phrase. We were assigned to bunks in a barrack. Very soon the grumbling about the sergeant began. Some of the soldiers were already feeling homesick and expressed the fear that army life was going to be too tough for them. They did not know what 'tough' was! So far, the demands made upon us did not present any difficulty for me.

Next day we had more orientation, and we were put on KP duty. KP is short for 'kitchen police', which means duty in the kitchen, any duty from cleaning pots and pans to serving on the food line. Nobody liked KP, so it was often used by the sergeants as impromptu punishment.

In the evenings, we went to a movie on post and, with the 'flying twenty', we could go to the PX, (the post exchange), the army's general store on base. There, we could purchase whatever we wanted. Food was plentiful, and I enjoyed choosing what I liked in the army kitchen. We were told that we could eat as much as we wanted, but that we should eat everything we took. No waste, please! This was a rule I could understand and very much appreciate. We were required to exercise every morning. For me, this army training was like summer camp, in comparison to the 'camps' I had experienced.

In personnel interviews, they took down more history and asked about my previous employment. I mentioned the jobs I had had, but I also said that I had some knowledge and experience in dental laboratory work. That information got me assigned to Camp Pickett, Virginia, the Army's medical training center.

They had a chinning bar in front of the barracks where we lined up before each meal. We were supposed to do twenty-five pull-ups on it; however, none of us was in condition to do that many, but we had to do as many as possible before we went to the mess hall for our breakfast.

The training schedule called for sixteen weeks, eight for basic and eight for medical training. One night during the first week of the basic training phase, the sergeant came into the barracks just before we turned in. He kept us up until two in the morning telling us all kinds of stories. We believed that he did this on purpose, since we were told that we would usually get no more than four or five hours of sleep a night during our training. We were up by five o'clock that morning in our fatigues and on the pull-up bar.

Now the training really got underway. The first couple of weekends there were no passes. After that, a pass depended on how well you came through Saturday morning inspection. Everything had to be right: shoes and belt buckles polished like mirrors, beds made so tight a quarter would bounce on them, footlockers arranged by the diagram in the manual, clothes racks neat to a fault, windows and floors spotless. That routine was not easy to master, and weekend passes in the early weeks of were scarce.

In the first few weeks, many of us could not pass inspection, because we did not have the time to meet the standards of care for our personal belongings; even when the barracks were up to snuff. The sergeant wrote down all the criticisms and, if there were too many, no passes for anyone. After one bad experience getting caught hanging around the barracks on the weekend and being sent on KP duty, I always went to the library or to a movie or found some other way to keep busy and returned to quarters only to sleep.

Army basic training consisted of learning army methods in the use of field and combat equipment. You soon heard that in all things, there was a wrong way, a right way and an army way. We went through training on the rifle and machine gun ranges, the grenade range, the gas shed, the infiltration course, mines and booby traps, night marches, day marches and bivouacs. We got it all and it was tough, very tough, but a different kind of tough from what I had known from the camps in Poland and Germany.

In the third week, we had to learn how to be prepared against a gas attack. We were taken to a small building in which the training cadre had readied some kind of stink bomb or tear gas. We had to enter that building without a gas mask. As we were to enter, the gas bomb would be set off. One look at the situation terrified me, because it brought back all those horrible memories of the Auschwitz gas chambers where my mother probably died.

I ran over to Corporal Parrot and blurted out my fear. He was immediately sympathetic and said he was not aware of that side of my story. He explained firmly that in army training, as in the combat for which we were being made ready, there were no exceptions and no excuses. Everyone must go through the same training; everyone must pass through that building, gas and all. He assured me I would come through it fine and nothing bad would happen to me. I saw the others come out rubbing their eyes and coughing, and it took all my courage and more to go in there. But I did. When I emerged, I was shaking from head to toe. Corporal Parrot came over to me and said, "I knew you could do it, and I am very proud of you." I was proud of me too, but to this day, for obvious reasons, I will not enter a steam bath.

When winter came, we started the medical phase of our basic training, which included a lot of first aid. They paired us up, and we went into the woods, each of us carrying half a pup tent. This exercise was to teach us survival in harsh weather conditions. I bunked with a fellow recruit named Robert Sklar from Connecticut. We had a small can filled with candle wax which we were told to light for a little heat. They issued raincoats and more blankets, and trucks brought us hot food. This exercise lasted for a week. Although conditions were by no means pleasant, I rather liked the idea that these exercises would toughen me, this time in a positive way.

When we finished basic training, I received an assignment to the Madigan Army Hospital at Fort Lewis, Washington near Tacoma. I had been awarded the military occupation specialty (MOS) of laboratory technician in the Army Medical Corps. I was given a reporting date and a thirty-day leave.

The family was very happy to see me after the six-months' absence. In the time I had, I visited my relatives and all the people I knew. Mike Rosenfeld and I went to dances, movies and the theater. I even called on the employer who had fired me from my first job in New York. He was surprised—pleasantly, I thought—to see me and commented that I was looking very well. For this occasion, I had worn my army uniform. He brought up the refrigerator incident and apologized for losing his temper. I said that I was sorry to have insulted him. He took me in the back of the shop to show me that he had purchased a new refrigerator for the employees.

We said good-bye, and I felt good having mended fences.

I was also able to help Tibor with the medical bills incurred by his daughter Kathryn's illness, because I had saved money from my army pay. He was very thankful, since her medication was quite expensive.

Several days before my leave was up, I had to start for Fort Lewis—a four-day trip coast to coast. The train I took carried a lot of army personnel and since we were all going in the same direction, we stayed together. The seating accommodations were fine, but since there were no sleeping cars, we had to spend the nights on benches. The dining car was our favorite hangout. When we finally arrived at the Tacoma station, we were met by army transport trucks for the twenty-mile trip to Madigan Hospital at Fort Lewis.

At the hospital, we were given an orientation and assigned to billets in a comfortable two-story building. We were fifteen to a room, each with his own bunk. It was great not to be in barracks. A civilian contractor was hired to keep the building clean. We had no inspections. What luxury!

During the day, we wore hospital-issue white uniforms and at night, we could change into civvies (civilian clothes). On our time off, we were free to stay on the base, go to a movie, go into the city, pretty much whatever we wished to do. I often went to Seattle, because we were invited by some of the families for breakfast or dinner, and we also spent the Jewish holidays with these families. On such holidays, we had the day off and switched duties with our colleagues of the Christian faith, and we did the same for them at Christmas time.

Another fellow and I visited a very nice Jewish family. The father was an attorney who had been born in Ireland. His children were fascinated with our army uniforms. We all gathered around and he told stories about the war years in England when London was bombed. I told about my experiences and he was astonished by my story. He had heard a little about the camps and what had happened in Europe, but he did not know too much and had never met a survivor.

This particular family treated us royally. After several visits, they tried to convince me to come back to Seattle when my military tour was completed. They said they would provide me with help and support. As much as I liked them and the city, I did not think that such a move would be the right thing for me. I simply told them that I could not make a decision at that time.

On the weekend, when we went into Seattle, the Jewish organization offered us wonderful breakfasts— pancakes, lox, bagels, the works. Three of the guys from Camp Pickett wound up at Fort Lewis. They were Dick Ayres, Kenneth Voght and Raymond Augustus. They loved to go to breakfast with me. The four of us were together a lot, and we became good army buddies, although they worked in different departments of the hospital.

I was in the dental clinic with a Colonel Kelly in charge. He was a good person and after he got to know me, he wrote a letter of recommendation for me in preparation for the time when I would apply for citizenship with the Naturalization/Immigration Department. I enjoyed working in the clinic where I worked with various dentists. I also spent a little time in the dental laboratory. When it came to surgery, that was a different story-- too much blood. When I asked to be transferred out of that area, they did it with no problem.

I was transferred to work with Colonel Lafitte, a dentist from Wisconsin, who also turned out to be a nice person. I enjoyed working for him, although he had a habit of not wanting a minute wasted. On occasion Colonel Lafitte's over-zealous work habits produced bizarre consequences. One day, a soldier came in from another department with some papers under his arm. He was standing around waiting when the Colonel shouted at him. "Sit down and don't waste my time." The soldier was so startled that he sat down and immediately received a shot on both sides of his mouth. "Tell me what hurts," the Colonel demanded. The soldier stammered, "Nothing hurts. I did not come here about my teeth. I have papers for you to sign." The Colonel apologized and told the soldier not to worry -- that the shots would wear off within half an hour. Then he signed the papers and the befuddled soldier left. We could hardly contain ourselves until the soldier had gone, and then both of us almost collapsed with laughter.

Colonel Lafitte asked a lot of questions about my past, and we hit it off very well. My duties were to sterilize and prepare the instruments he used when patients came in for treatment. I learned a lot about dentistry there, but I was not much in the laboratory which as I have mentioned, was my specialty. I worked with the Colonel quite some time before I was finally assigned to the dental laboratory. I found out that the army always puts people where they are needed without much regard for their training.

On Saturdays, when officers' dependents came in t the office, some of the wives that were pregnant, had to be treated very carefully. They were always given a glass of water with a pill, which made them drowsy. By the time they came into the treatment room, they were so relaxed it was easy to work on them. I met some nice people there on Saturday mornings, including some attractive girls. I also became acquainted with the officers and their families.

One day when I had about twelve months left to go on my two-year army stint, I was called to report to a certain building on the post. About ten other soldiers were there, all originally from foreign countries. The sergeant in charge told us we were to take a language test. We were put in separate cubicles with a phonograph. I was required to interpret from Hungarian to English and from German to English. The questionnaire took over an hour to complete. After they collected and reviewed the tests, the sergeant read out our names for assignments to different parts of the world. When he came to my name, he smiled and said, "You did very well on the language test, and you are being shipped overseas."

I wondered what part of Germany I would be sent to, since the army still had a majority of its bases there. To my surprise, the sergeant said, "You are being sent to Pusan, Korea." I asked him, "What should I do with Hungarian and German in Korea? Now they are sending me where neither of those languages is spoken. Why did they bother to give me a language test?" By this time, I knew not to expect an answer, and I did not get one. But the sergeant had a smirk on his face when he told me that I had a thirty day leave before I was to report to the embarkation point in Seattle.

I was still confused by what had happened, so I had to inquire further and found out that my MOS number called for a dental technician in Korea to replace someone, and this requirement took precedence over my knowledge of European languages. I was not excited about going to Korea, even though the hostilities there were coming to an end. There was still a lot of guerrilla-type warfare going on, but mainly, I had heard that it was not a very nice place for foreigners. Once again, I had no choice.

I took my furlough. The army provided transportation to Ohio where I caught a plane to New York. It was the beginning of January 1953 when I arrived in New York. My brother and family were very pleased to have me home. I visited with all the people I knew, went out a lot and enjoyed my leave as much as possible.

Then I went back to Seattle, where I reported at the embarkation point. We were processed and given inoculations for Korea. The ship for Pusan arrived a few days later and about 3,000 of us were boarded, along with 100 South Korean army officers who had received training in the US.

Our quarters were below decks where the diesel smell was strong, and we slept in hammocks. I asked how rough was the Pacific Ocean, since I was remembering all too

well my first ocean voyage to the US. I was assured that this trip would be much calmer; however, this forecast was not too accurate. The boat started rocking from time to time and once again I became very seasick. To top it off, breakfast was at 6:00 am and, although regular breakfast food was served, they also had franks and beans. One whiff and I was in trouble. Fortunately, the ocean calmed just before lunchtime and almost immediately I felt better. Luckily it stayed fairly calm the remainder of the trip over. I tried to stay on deck during the day, since there were no duties, and we had only occasional drills because I felt much better when I was higher up on the ship.

I remember one day when I heard Eddy Fisher's recording of "Oh, My Papa", and it affected me so profoundly that I ran to the railing of the ship and felt tears running down my face. Such a feeling of sadness came over me and I thought, "Here I am free and healthy, and lucky to be living in the USA with my whole life ahead of me. My poor parents and Izidor—why did their lives end too soon and in such horrible ways? Why did these things happen to good people?" But, as always, there were no answers.

Six days later, we sailed into Yokohama harbor, Japan. What a difference from the three-week trip crossing the Atlantic to the US.

Korea

As we came close to Yokohama harbor, the people on the dock looked like ants scurrying around, since the ship was many stories high. The captain had his work cut out for him maneuvering that ship into port with another ship going out at the same time. The clearance between the two was so close that it seemed as though we could reach out and touch the people on the other ship.

After we docked, we transferred onto a smaller ship that took us to Pusan harbor in Korea. When we arrived there, it appeared as though we had reached an entirely different world. The worst was the smell, which was nauseating. We could not imagine what could cause such an odor. We later learned that the awful stench which greeted us was human feces used as fertilizer by the rice farmers.

The American military had tried to build up the harbor, but it was still very run down. As we disembarked, we realized the weather was freezing. We found out that the cold air comes down directly from Siberia onto the Korean peninsula. There was an army band to welcome us, which seemed a little strange in the surroundings. The army had trucks lined up to take us to a temporary camp for the night. As soon as we arrived at the camp, we were lined up for chow, and then they handed out about six blankets apiece. They told us the nights were extremely cold and we would need every one of them. This was no exaggeration.

The next morning, a group of Korean children came to the camp begging for chocolate and chewing gum, but we had nothing to give them. The following day, those of us who were assigned to the 21st Station Hospital were loaded onto trucks. A section of the hospital was supposed to be a mobile dental unit which traveled around treating army personnel; however, the "mobile" dental unit turned out to be in a barrack, and that is where we were located.

The barrack to which we were assigned consisted of aluminum huts, and they were cold—we were cold. We were assigned to bunks, fed chow and then we received the inevitable orientation. I was to work in the dental laboratory. Our mission was to treat United Nations (UN) personnel coming in from the front lines, as well as soldiers who had injuries to their teeth.

There were about ten of us in the lab. I became friends with Bernie Buchalter from Detroit, and a fellow from San Diego named Hutchinson. We worked long hours because we were the only dental laboratory in the area, and there was much to be done. A Major Lovelace was the officer in charge, and I worked with him in the clinic. I learned a lot more about dentistry under Lovelace and became his right hand man. Soon after my arrival he announced that he would be going home in a month - to be replaced by someone else. I was sorry to see him go.

Lt. Morrison from Tampa, Florida took over and he asked me to work with him, since I now had the experience. Morrison was not as easygoing as Lovelace had been, and he increased the number of patients we handled in a day. He also gave me the additional job of scheduling appointments, which took up so much time that it was like having two jobs.

However, I did not mind because Lt. Morrison was kind to us and, on Sundays, he loaned us his jeep and driver. We took picnic lunches with us and visited some of the Buddhist Temples and other interesting sights in the area.

We were repeatedly warned about the various diseases we could contract if we were not extremely careful. We were also cautioned to be especially wary of mosquitoes, which carry sickness. At night, we slept in tents, and there was a stink bomb in the center of the aluminum hut to ward off insects. Once I was bitten by a mosquito and had to get eight shots, four on each arm, because the threat was so dangerous.

There was not too much to do in Pusan. When we went down to the port to pick up our supplies for the clinic, I noticed some European army officers, one from Czechoslovakia and one from Poland. They told us that, since the war had ended, they were assigned to see what equipment came into port. In the northern sector, there were Swiss and Swedish officers doing the same duty, since the conflict was a UN operation. I noticed other personnel from different countries—Turks, Ethiopians,

Australians, British. All of them had been in the conflict against North Korea and later, China.

Once, we were invited by some Turks for coffee as a gesture of gratitude for taking care of their teeth. They were rough-looking soldiers with bayonets on their belts. I was glad to be considered their ally. The occasion was my first experience drinking Turkish coffee. It was so thick you could almost cut it with a knife and I actually found it hard to swallow. However, we had been advised not to refuse anything offered, as a refusal would be taken as an insult. We also became friendly with some Dutch soldiers with whom we played Ping-Pong, and they were very pleasant company. In the lab, I also met people from all over the world who had come to Korea to fight Communist North Korea.

The army mess was not as good as in the states because, with the conflict over, fewer supplies came in. Sometimes, we went to the Chinese Nationalist (Taiwan) Embassy, bribed the cook with cigarettes and had dinner there. That food was very good. We were cautioned not to go to any Korean restaurants because they were not very clean at that time. We were also warned to be very careful if we associated with Korean women, because venereal diseases were running rampant. Life was quite restricted in Korea during the time we were there.

We did meet Korean officers in the clinic and some of them invited us to their homes. We always had a good time, but I was squeamish about the food served and ate mostly vegetables. Food was very scarce at the time, and the Koreans supplemented their menus with items that were very questionable; particularly the meat that was used.

When it came to the Jewish high holidays, there was a rabbi from England who held services. We had a little wine and matzos and Passover food was provided from the states. We did the best we could.

R&R in Japan

After six months, we were ready for R and R (rest and recreation). We had two choices: either to go overnight to Japan or to be taken by submarine to Hong Kong. Although Hong Kong sounded enticing, memories of my two sea voyages convinced me not to try a trip on a submarine, so I chose Japan and my friends agreed.

Our destination was Kyoto, which was the old capital of Japan, and a very cultural city. At this time, they were in the midst of the Cherry Festival. The hotel reserved by the army was the Rakuyo. Each meal would cost us only 25¢, which would be used as a tip for the hotel workers. They told us to wear our fatigues on the ship over, but to take our army dress uniforms with us.

We arrived the following day at Kobe, changed into our uniforms and, from there, we took a train. We passed through Osaka on the way to Kyoto and to our hotel. There were four of us, two in a room. Since we were good buddies, we decided that, whatever we did, we would do together. We started our week's vacation that evening in the hotel dining room, which was quite beautiful. An orchestra was playing, and the meal was delicious. Music was being played again the next morning when we went for breakfast. We had a choice of anything our hearts desired, and the food was just as good as the night before.

After breakfast, we went to a very interesting department store, a place that was ahead of its time. On the roof was a nursery for children who were taken care of by competent help while their parents or chaperones shopped.

After a lovely dinner, we walked all over the city. Everyone was very polite and helpful to us. The next day we visited a big palace, which was painted black on the top and inlaid with gold plate. They told us it was formerly the Emperor's palace. We found fascinating places to visit, and the Cherry Festival was very beautiful.

One night, all four of us wound up in a bar attended by bar girls whom we found out were either students or had other jobs. They were decent girls who wanted companionship and nothing more. We had a few drinks and got acquainted. Later on, one of the girls invited all of us to her house, which was large and comfortable. We spent a very nice evening and stayed there for the night. Next morning, they took us sightseeing, and we spent a couple of days with them, enjoying ourselves very much. Because they had gone out of their way to be so hospitable, we wanted to compensate them in some way, but we did not want to offend them. We tried to explain in English that, since it was a Japanese custom to give a gift when entertained, we wished to show our gratitude for their generous hospitality. So we put some money in an envelope, which we gave them and they appreciated it. We said good-bye and tried to decide what to do with our remaining days.

We heard about the Japanese inns outside the city which were very restful and relaxing, but they warned us that there was no radio or television at these places. We reasoned that, if it was relaxation we were looking for, one of those inns would be perfect; especially with a

Japanese hot bath. We decided to try one and made reservations.

We spent two days at the inn and slept on the floor on a tatami, which is a bamboo bed. During the day, we went through the hot bath routine. First, I had to shower, and then the bath. When I came out, I was surprised when one of the Japanese women who worked there came toward me with a big bucket and threw ice water over me. My body nearly went into shock. The woman smiled very discreetly, hiding her mouth behind her fingers, since it was considered impolite to display too much laughter. After that, there was a wonderful massage. It was all delightful and relaxing as promised.

After the two days were over, we left the inn feeling great. We had one more day left and took a cab back to the Hotel Rakuyo, where we went to the bar and had a few drinks. A few turned out to be too many for me because I was unaccustomed to drinking hard liquor. I could not stand up straight, and my friends had to support me out of the bar.

The next day, the roster was called, and we had to prepare to go back to Pusan. We changed back into our fatigues and took the train to Kobe, then the ship to Korea. After our wonderful week of R&R in Kyoto, Japan, Korea did not look very good to us.

Back to the States

I was in my 23rd month in the army, when I received orders to prepare to return to the states. Two of my friends had to remain in Korea because they had not finished their two year tour of duty. We all promised to get in contact when they returned to the states. Ed Feinberg and I left on a small ship to the Yokohama harbor, where about 4,000 troops were boarding the ship back to the states. Since each name was called as people boarded, we did not leave until the following day.

I was determined on this trip to find a way to avoid sleeping in the bottom of this very large ship and risk getting seasick again. It occurred to me after we boarded that the ship would have a dentist. I asked Ed to watch my duffel bag while I ran all the way up to the top deck where the ship's medical doctor and a dentist were located. I told the Marine guard who was standing at attention there, that I wanted to see the dentist. He told me that this was an off-limits area and asked if I had a toothache. I told him the reason I wanted to see the dentist was not about my teeth, but to volunteer my services since I had worked in the dental unit in Pusan. He asked me to wait.

In a few minutes, the dentist came rushing out and introduced himself as Lt. John Lewis. He said, "Come inside, I want to talk to you. Where is your equipment and duffel bag?" I told him my buddy was watching them and he told me to get them and come right back. I ran down all the steps and told Ed what had happened. I said that I did not know if I would be able to see him again during the trip because I was going to try and work out something with the dentist. Ed promised to visit me in the dental office, and so I gathered my things and once again ran back up to the top deck.

The Marine guard took me into the office. The dentist laughed because I was so red in the face from running up and down the steps. He asked me what I could do and told me there were over 4,000 GIs plus officers with only three or four Navy men who worked in the dental unit. Everyone's teeth were supposed to be cleaned and there were not enough people on hand to do the job. He said he could use my help and showed me a bunk in the dental supply room where I could sleep. He explained that I could stay on the top deck and would never have to go below. If I could give him the help he so desperately needed, then the arrangements could be worked out to our mutual benefit.

As to the matter of learning how to clean teeth, which I had never done, Lt. Lewis said, "Okay, today you will watch the Navy Medical Corps people, and they will explain and show you everything. Tomorrow you will start cleaning teeth. We have to do as many as we can." He showed me the supply room, gave me a white jacket and took me to watch the others work. He told me that, when it was lunch time, I should follow the people to whom I was attached, instead of going to the mess hall. He showed me the shower facilities and, although the bunk was small, I was happy just to be on the top deck, where I knew from past experience that, even if I felt a little queasy, it would definitely be much better than being in the bottom of the ship.

The next day, I watched the other corpsmen, who explained each of the instruments, how they were used, and how to take care of them. They suggested that I practice on someone that afternoon. I told them I would rather watch some more. I was quite worried about handling those sharp instruments with so little instruction and no practice. They told me not to be concerned because you get used to it very quickly. But watching and doing were quite different, as I found out the following day. I watched what they did very carefully, and everyone was very helpful. Obviously, they had been instructed by Lt. Lewis to teach me as much as possible in as short a time as possible.

When we went to eat, we received the same food as the officers in a small attractive dining room. I felt lucky to be in such a good situation, which made me determined to put in as much effort as I could to do a good job. That night we watched a movie in a small projection room and were served ice cream. Although I was only a private first class, I continued to receive the same treatment as the officers. The dentist said that I was doing him a favor by helping him, and I knew that he was doing me a favor by providing me with a good way in which to avoid being seasick.

The next day, I was terrified at the thought of cleaning anyone's teeth on my own. I felt very nervous and my hands were shaking. An orderly came in and announced my first patient. In came a sergeant who thanked me in advance for being able to do this for him. His very words made me tremble. I wondered if he would still thank me when I had finished. I started to work and proceeded to cut his gum, then his lip. He started to bleed, and finally he pointed out that there seemed to be a lot of blood. I told him not to worry, that the bleeding was part of the process; he should rinse his mouth with cold water and it would stop. He rinsed and rinsed, but it was some time before the bleeding stopped.

After the sergeant left, I waited a few minutes to try to calm myself. When my next patient sat down in the chair, I was still very tense and my hands were shaking, but I tried to be more careful. However, this one also bled quite a bit before he escaped my hands. The next one was a little better, and by the time I had done five or six cleanings, I was almost expert at the procedure. I did the cleanings for about a week; ten or twelve each day. The dentist commented, "You are doing a beautiful job. How about signing up for the Navy before you get your discharge?" I thanked him but declined the offer, saying that I was looking forward to going home and becoming a civilian once again, and he said he understood.

Civilian Life, and getting My Citizenship

We arrived in New York Harbor and went to Camp Kilmer for final processing. I received my honorable discharge, my mustering out pay and my savings. Another friend and I took the bus from New Jersey and the subway back to Brooklyn. We talked all the way about our lives in the army and how good it was to be back. We agreed that we were both lucky to be returning from Korea in good health.

When I arrived at Tibor's apartment, he was at work, but my sister-in-law and the girls were happy to see me. Kathryn, however, was terribly ill. I was shocked to see her looking so thin and sickly. The cystic fibrosis had progressed to the point where the doctors could no longer help her. It was a rather sad homecoming.

Later that evening, Tibor and I sat and talked. After a while, he handed me a letter from Tema.

It was written in Hebrew, and so it took a while until I could unscramble it. I finally understood that she was asking me to contact her when I returned from the army. Tema said she looked forward to continuing our friendship. She was living in Brooklyn, not too far from us. At this point, I found myself hesitant to resume the relationship because her father and family, as I remembered, were extremely religious. I had seen how the Orthodox Jews in Brooklyn lived, and it was very strange to me and I had no desire to conduct my life that way.

I had to go to the Veterans Administration to register and find out about the benefits available to me. When I got there the next day, the first thing they told me was that I had to go to 1st Army Headquarters to sign up for a required eight years in the enlisted reserve. That meant that, if any national emergency occurred in which I was needed during that enlistment, I would be called to active duty. This news came as a surprise, as I did not recall hearing about that obligation in any of the induction briefings.

I qualified for my American citizenship the year after I was discharged from the army. The day I was sworn in, March 18, 1955, was a proud one for me. I had served in the United States Army for two years and so I thought of myself as an American, but I did not become one until the moment I pledged allegiance to the American Constitution and the American flag.

On that day, the judge who granted us our citizenship, gave us a break for lunch and announced that those of us who would like to change our names could do this as part of the citizenship proceedings when we returned to his chambers. I decided then and there that I wanted to change my name though I had never given it a thought until that moment. With so little time available to make this decision, I rushed to the nearest telephone booth and looked in the directory under the "S" names and came across "Simpson". For some strange reason, that name sounded right to me, and after translating Gyuri to George, that is how I became George Simpson.

The same night I called Tema who was not home. Her father told me to come over to their house, since she would be returning shortly. Tema's mother and sister were there too. They told me she was attending night school, and while I waited, they served cake and coffee. Although they were friendly enough, I felt rather uncomfortable and wondered what I was getting myself into.

In a little while, Tema showed up and came over and gave me a hug and a kiss on the cheek. We talked for over an hour. She asked me if we could renew our friendship, go out a bit and see what developed. For a while after that first meeting, things seemed to be going nicely. Then Tema's father started to question me about my religious beliefs and I admitted to him that I was not a very religious person. He also asked me about my future, the answer to which I did not have at that time. Her father said it was a shame that I was not orthodox because Tema really liked me and the family liked me. I felt the noose tightening. Soon after this conversation, I noticed a sudden coolness on his part. Tema and I discussed the situation, and she acknowledged that she was as religious as her parents and intended to live her life in an orthodox manner. I told her I did not and could not feel that way, and a very sad expression came across her face.

I asked if we could continue our friendship, but her answer was evasive. I let the situation cool. When I called her a week or so later, she was not home, and I was not able to reach her for a while. When I finally did, I could hear the aloofness in her voice. All traces of our former friendship in Paris were gone. I had a sense of guilt, because I could not be the person Tema wanted me to be. We met once more and it was obvious to me that the relationship was over. I felt quite downhearted by this turn of events.

My friend, Mike, and I discussed the situation, and he suggested that it would take a little time, but when I started dating others; in due time, I would get over the disappointment and be able to get Tema out of my mind. Eventually, I did start dating again.

Since I was still living in Tibor's house, my social life posed some problems between us. Very often, Tibor asked me to go with him to the synagogue on Saturday when I had already made other plans. Also, we had strictly Kosher food at home, and he did not like the restaurants I frequented or the fact that I wanted to eat out so often. I began to feel very restricted and resented always having to defend my choices.

I had stayed in the apartment with Tibor and his family, because I had a lot to think about before I decided what to do. I knew that I should move out on my own, but I did not know whether to go back to work or use the GI bill for school and resume my education. Whatever I decided, I knew the time had come to start my life as an independent person. However, I did not want to rush these decisions because I wanted to make the right choices.

Tibor and I continued to discuss ideas that might lead to a business partnership between us. I brought one such idea home with me from Japan. When I was on leave there, I happened upon a store, which sold beautiful silkscreen pictures of the Japanese scenery. I had sent some to Tibor and he liked the pictures very much and said he thought we could do something with them. When I returned home, Tibor suggested that we write to the company that manufactured them and find out what other kinds of pictures they had. We contacted the Japanese Chamber of Commerce and learned the name of the manufacturer.

Meantime, I went back to the quilting factory where I had worked before my military service. The aim was to make some immediate money while deciding, based on availability of veteran's benefits, what I was going to do and which school I would choose. I was welcomed back to the company in New Jersey. The wages had gone up, and I started making good money. Tibor, who was still with that company, brought in some of the pictures from Japan and showed them to a Puerto Rican fellow who worked there. He became very interested. He had the idea of making religious pictures on silkscreen, and he gave us an example, "The Last Supper". He asked if I thought this could be done because there was a large market in Puerto Rico for such pictures. I did not know the answer, but suggested we send examples of what we had in mind to Japan. The Japanese manufacturer sent back illustrations of what they could do, and these samples were exactly what we wanted.

We ordered some to be sent to a dealer in Puerto Rico, who carried religious articles. They were an immediate and huge success. This business went on for over a year; however, since a lot of people were involved, and the profits had to be divided so many ways, no one made a great deal of money. It was necessary that we all continue our jobs at the factory.

We started to order some pictures of New York scenery and sold them to the Woolworth Company. This move looked promising. But, after a short time, the Woolworth people found out where the pictures were manufactured and made their own deal to buy them directly. This intervention knocked us out of the business. Had we been more experienced, we might have done something to protect our interests.

After some thought, I decided to resume my dental laboratory studies. I had heard that crown and bridgework, especially porcelain work, was of a very high quality and in great demand. If I should eventually decide not to pursue that specialty, I could always go back and learn something else. I started to think again about my childhood dream to be a pediatrician, but I did not know if I should attempt such an undertaking at this late stage, (I was almost 28 years old) since the training would take many years before I would become a practicing physician. So I went to night school to qualify as a dental technician, and during the day, I worked at my regular job.

Marriage and Divorce

While still in New York, I entered into a marriage with a woman named Suzi, that would not work out so well, so once again, I made arrangements to break up the life I had established, looking for a complete change of scenery, and when those arrangements had been made, a friend named Mike drove me to the airport. Suzi had stepped out on me with other men, and her parents were quite embarrassed by the whole thing. Suzi's parents had given me the name and address of some friends in Los Angeles, the Carmels, where I could stay for a while. When I arrived in LA, before I met with them, I went first to a small hotel in their area.

These friends of Suzi's parents knew the whole sad story of my marriage. They suggested that, for the time being, I stay with them. They also assured me that, if I had any problems, I should talk things over with them and they would try to help me. They recommended an attorney, Earl Korchak, so that I could file for a divorce.

Eventually, the attorney notified Suzi, and she came to LA, so that we could go to Korchak's office and sign the papers. The divorce was granted in December 1963 without any complications because there were no children and few assets.

I had been very sad about not having children after several years of marriage; however, this type of subject was not so openly discussed then, but I always wondered why it never happened. But, having no children turned out to have been for the best under the circumstances. I was heartbroken over the whole situation because I had never contemplated that there would be a divorce in my life. It seemed like a failure, regardless of whose fault it was. Later on, I realized that friends had tried to hint that Suzi was not the person she appeared to be when we first married, but I suppose I was so eager to have a family that I just did not want to recognize that anything was wrong. I had made a huge mistake, but I was determined to learn from it. I knew that when I married again—and I was certain I would—that person would be someone quite different from Suzi.

I found a job in a dental laboratory, but when the people found out I wanted to specialize, they suggested that I should try a much bigger laboratory in downtown Los Angeles, which I did.

I bought a new car and continued to live with the Carmel family as a paying guest since the rent was low. A short time later, I decided I wanted to be on my own, so I rented a room and bath in a private house from a lady named Mrs. Barton. She had three or four other lodgers and the rent was quite reasonable.

As previously mentioned, my relationship with Tibor was not close. When I left New York, we were not on speaking terms, so I did not tell him I was leaving. But soon after I arrived in LA, I wrote to let him know where I was. He eventually answered, but the tone of his letter was distant and not at all supportive of my attempts to make a new life.

I started dating, and after a little more than a year, I still had not found anyone I could think seriously about. It seemed that LA was a city where I could have good times, but it did not appear to be the place where I could find that special person. I became very frustrated, and told Mrs. Barton that I might be going back to New York. I thought that perhaps now I would be luckier there, but I could not make up my mind whether to go - or stay. I was certainly no longer the same person who left New York, and now I knew that if I were to go back, I would have to travel in different circles than before.

As I was getting ready to pack my things, still somewhat undecided as to whether or not to leave, I received a telephone call from an acquaintance named Aranka Wald who knew me through the Carmels. She said she would like to introduce me to a very nice lady that she had met recently. She told me that, although she did not like to play the role of matchmaker, she had grown very fond of this person and had a feeling that I would like her. I said that I did not particularly care for blind dates and since I might be going back to New York, there did not seem to be any point in it. Aranka was very persuasive and said that this was a very special person in her opinion, but even if nothing came of it, an evening out would not be unpleasant. Then she mentioned that Helene had two small children and I said that would not matter. So she gave me Helene's telephone number. I was quite skeptical and wondered if I should even bother to call. After all, I had one foot out of California, but then curiosity got the best of me.

A New Life

One evening during that week, I happened to be in the Park LaBrea shopping center, when I decided to call Helene. I remember the phone booth and to this day, whenever I pass there, I think about that night which was a turning point in my life. We spoke for over a half hour, exchanging little bits of information, and the call went smoothly between us. I felt something click. I asked when I could see her and if she had a preference as to where we should go. She said any place would be fine where we could sit and talk since we didn't know each other. That made sense to me, and so I chose the elegant and beautiful Bel Air Hotel that had a cocktail lounge with a fireplace and a pianist. That is where we had our first date.

Two nights later, a Thursday evening, when I called for Helene, my first impression was that she was extremely tall, but when she came toward me, I realized that she was actually a medium height. As we shook hands in greeting, she looked at me with dark brown soulful eyes and I felt everything melt inside of me. She was more than pretty and I was strongly attracted right then and there. We talked non-stop for hours in the romantic atmosphere at the Hotel Bel Air, and had such a good time, that we made a date for the next Saturday. We went to a seafood restaurant on the Pacific Coast Highway for dinner and by the time that evening was over, I knew she was going to be someone very special to me. Thoughts of leaving California disappeared, and I immediately decided to unpack for the time being.

The next week, Helene invited me to her home for dinner. She turned out to be a great cook and I had a good time with her children, Janet and Michael. We began to see each other several times a week, and very soon it became almost every day. On Sundays, we all went out for the day and each time we went to a different place. The children would get into the car, and when we approached our destination, I would tell them to close their eyes and it would be places like Disneyland, Knotts Berry Farm, or horseback riding at Griffith Park. I had fun planning those surprise excursions, and they began to feel like real family outings. I could see that Helene was relaxed and happy because both her children took to me and enjoyed being with us and we all had such a good time.

A few months went by like this, and I was sure that I was in love with Helene, so I asked her to marry me, and she said yes. Shortly after that, we had our first serious quarrel! For no reason I can give, it came to my mind that I would like to have a Kosher home. I asked Helene if she would do that for me. To her everlasting credit, she refused. In a remarkable replay of my own earlier thoughts which I had felt so strongly in New York, she said that she did not wish to live the kind of restricted life required by any rigid religious customs. She explained that, growing up, she had friends from different circles, and before she was widowed, her life had been filled with travel and association with people from all over the US and Europe. She said, "This is who I am, and if I am not what you want as I am, then we are not right for each other." At first, I was angry and disappointed, but in a very cool manner, Helene told me to think about it, and I did.

The more I thought about my request, the more I realized that I was asking Helene for something I myself had not wanted to do for Tema, or for that matter, for my brother, Tibor. I said to myself, "George, what are you doing? What is this really all about, now that you have found the person you have been looking for? You know you love her. Are you about to lose her being stubborn about something you probably don't even really want?" I was confused. Finally Helene and I talked again, and we came to the conclusion that perhaps this had something to do with my family who had not survived. My parents had been quite religious and had lost their lives because of their beliefs, and now I was unwilling to practice the rules and regulations of our religion in their memory. After much thought and consideration, of one thing I was certain, I was not willing to lose Helene.

One weekend after this issue was settled, we took the children to San Diego, and on the beach, Janet and Michael each took me by a hand and asked me to go for a walk. As we walked along, Janet, the older of the two, said, "Would you mind if we called you Daddy, now that you are going to marry us?" My eyes filled with tears. I could not think of anything better than being their daddy. The three of us became quite emotional, and they ran back to their mother to tell her. She was smiling, because they had talked it over with her first. I always wanted them to remember their biological father, who had died quite suddenly of an illness a few years earlier, but for me, this was the beginning of my family and now they would be my children too.

On June 7, 1964, about seven months after we met, Helene and I were married, and her parents were there from New York. Helene had quite a few relatives living in California and we both had friends, so we had planned a nice afternoon wedding with about 75 people in attendance. Since Aranka, the person who introduced us was orthodox and I expected Tibor to be there, we arranged for the food to be kosher. I called Tibor to invite him to the wedding, but he refused to come. I was very hurt because I wanted someone from my family to share this time with me. Then he shocked me even further, by asking why of all things, was I marrying a woman with two children. He said, "I think you could do better than that." I was so angry that I hung up on him. I was no longer a boy, but a man of 35 years, and so happy to have found the person with whom I knew I wanted to spend my life and two wonderful children in the bargain. Although Tibor and I met once in New York a few years later, we have been estranged since that time.

After the wedding, we left on our honeymoon for Hawaii. Helene's parents stayed in the apartment with the children. Honolulu was very enjoyable and we visited the islands of Maui and Kauai, which were very beautiful. We had a wonderful time and came home after a week, relaxed and ready to make some important decisions.

Now I had to decide once and for all what my professional future would be. Helene tried to convince me to go to medical school to be a pediatrician, but I felt that it really was too late in my life to start a course of training that would take so many years to complete. And now I had a family! She told me the decision was mine and that she would go along with whatever I decided. I knew I would not continue as a dental technician because there was no money to be made in that field in the US. After looking into several different occupations, eventually, through an acquaintance of mine, I went into insurance and became a broker.

I arranged to adopt Janet and Michael who were eager to have the same name as their mother and myself. I knew that I finally had a family of my own . It was a great moment in my life.

On New Year's Eve 1964, we went out with some cousins of Helene's. While she and I were on the dance floor, I noticed that she looked exceptionally happy and her eyes were sparkling. When midnight came, bells started ringing, horns were blowing, and Helene turned to me and said very gravely, "Happy New Year from Janet, Happy New Year from Michael and Happy New Year from the new baby who will be here in August." Well, I was so stunned, I could not move. I looked at Helene in wonder, and she laughed as she said, "Yes, I am pregnant, you can believe it." I did not know whether to laugh, cry or shout. I was so happy and excited, I almost burst!

We were living in the apartment that Helene had been living in before we were married, and had begun looking for a larger place. Now we decided we wanted to purchase a house, and we had to move quickly, since August was not that far off. Before too long, we found a house suitable for us, since we were about to be a family of five. After the necessary renovation and purchase of things needed, we moved into our home in spring.

One August evening around midnight, I noticed Helene running from room to room tidying everything, putting things from one place to another. I told her, "You shouldn't be doing so much now. You should be resting. It's only one week before the baby is due."

"I can't help it. I am so restless that I can't stay in one place." Around midnight, she said she had back pains and told me that for her this was the sign that it was time. She said she never experienced the terrible kind of labor pains that most women have—just back aches. So we called the doctor, and he told us to go to the hospital.

When we arrived at Hollywood Presbyterian, they told us to go home, because Helene was not ready to give birth. However, our doctor was on his way and he knew from her past history that this was the real thing, so we stayed at the hospital.

When the nurse came in and put the stethoscope on Helene's stomach and asked me to listen, I will never forget those sounds. I thought I was listening to Niagara Falls. We passed the time pleasantly and a few hours later, they took her to the delivery room. I was in the waiting room with another father-to-be, who was pacing nervously. I must admit that I was nervous too and also a little frightened. I could not stop thinking about my niece, Kathryn, and the cystic fibrosis; even though our gynecologist had taken a test from me and assured us that I was not a carrier. My stomach was tied in knots.

A little after six o'clock on the morning of August 7, 1965, the nurse came to tell me that I could see my wife and meet my new son. When I saw Helene, the first thing she said was, "Look what I have for you." She was holding this beautiful little baby in her arms. Tears streamed down my face when I saw our son. He had blond hair and blue eyes (that stayed blue) and as I looked at him, I could clearly see my mother's face. We called him Eric.

Helene and I were concerned that Janet and Michael might feel some jealousy because of all the attention the new baby was receiving, but he turned out to be exciting and fun for them and they joined right in helping to take care of him. To this day, our three children have a close relationship. Uncle Eric is much loved by his nieces and nephews, Jonathan, Alexandra and Madeleine Ames and Miranda and Aaron Simpson, our five grandchildren. Everything I had longed for and vowed to make happen during all those dark and terrible days has become reality.

Epilogue

Thirty years later, in 1995, I was driving past the Simon Wiesenthal Center in Los Angeles, where I noticed a long line of students and teachers waiting to enter. I had passed the Center many times, but this time I felt an urge to go inside. The Simon Wiesenthal Center has a Museum of Tolerance dedicated to teaching against prejudice as it exists all over the world. The Center has a collection of documents and artifacts from the many concentration camps, and easily accessible computerized information from German and US archives. Tours are given continuously, and survivors of the Holocaust speak to the public six days a week.

On that day in 1995, I looked around and spoke with some of the docents and then decided to become a supporting member. I was invited to come back the following week and give my personal testimony of the Holocaust.

That testimony was a very emotional experience for me, since I had never spoken in any detail to anyone about the events described in this book. Also, the appearance before an audience of strangers was intimidating, since I had not done any public speaking before this time. After the first presentation, the Center asked me to appear there regularly for the benefit of its visitors. I became increasingly comfortable with each successive talk and the visitors who stopped to hear my testimony seemed intensely interested.

I go to the Center several times a week now, more than two years after that first presentation. I have met so many interesting people from various places; and some have even become friends. I have been invited to speak to groups throughout California; to students of all ages, to religious groups of all denominations, to various police departments, civic organizations and institutions. One of the most memorable experiences was at the 29th Palms Marine Corps base, where I was warmly received, having been a former serviceman in the United States Army.

Upon mature reflection, I had no choice when I was caught up in the appalling events of World War II, but I did have choices among the many roads I have traveled since that time. I made mistakes and learned from some of them. But had I indulged in self-pity, pessimism and anger, I would have denied myself opportunities of new beginnings—more than once. I am grateful for the faith and strength which enabled me ultimately to choose the roads which, in the end, led to the important things in my life, a family which gives me love and great pride and brings continuous joy, and life in a country which to me is the best in the world.

Entrance to Auschwitz

Inside Auschwitz now of what the barracks look like

Barrack 15, which was the actual one that my father was crammed into.

My father as a young child in Hungary

Dad wearing lederhosen

My grandmother Vilma Sauer

My father's older brother
IzIdor

Grandfather Sandor, Grandmother Vilma, Uncle IzIdor, Uncle Tibor, Dad

Dad on the far left in his Army days

Dad on the far left as a Dental Tech in his Army days.

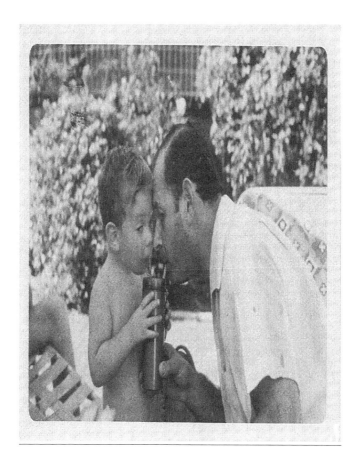

Dad and me in the
backyard of our first house

Mom and Dad on their Honeymoon

Dad, My brother Michael, My sister Janet, and little guy Me.

OTHER BOOKS WRITTEN
BY ERIC SIMPSON ARE

Displaced and Found

The Steps Along The Way

The Gifts of Experience
Due Date Spring of 2013

Made in the USA
Charleston, SC
07 September 2014